AF618657
9783954761722

actual
size

DISTANZ

Marlena Kudlicka

Artist pages

1 128

Index

120

Colophon

124

f=different
6

unprotected
0
34

shape hypothesis
test
66

Lecture as a
contour of A.
The beginning
of shape
90

a divided dot
100

The Differential Mystery
of Unprecedented Light
A Reading of Marlena
Kudlicka's Works

Octavio Zaya
110

Subtitle: Sculpture

Dorota Monkiewicz
114

The Measure of Decision

Miguel von Hafe Pérez
116

An Encounter with
Marlena Kudlicka

Friedrich Meschede
118

f=different	f=different	f=different	f=different
version 8,5:A4	f/To	9/9‘	3/1/1
2016, sculpture powdercoated steel glass 730 x 235 x 163 cm	2016, sculpture powdercoated steel glass 322 x 132 x 90 cm	2016 sculptural composition on wall powdercoated steel glass 210 x 300 x 10 cm	2016 sculpture powdercoated steel glass 250 x 225 x 30 cm

F
“f=different” series

In the new “f=different” series comprising sculptures and sculptural collages, I analyze and verify dependences between concepts of “different” and concepts of “standard”. The series title f=different refers to transition through different states whose incompleteness is caused by the aspect of error.
“f” is a durable unit, an axiom of uniform pattern and constant function.
“difference” signifies a group of various elements of a same value; it can also signify an equivalent that balances out the invariability of the function f. The concept of difference points towards certain topics such as Quality Control and Standard Verification.
In my recent series of works from 2016, I investigate the history of DIN A4 paper, and how its related idea of standard affects the relationship between linguistic and behavioral mechanisms. Through this curiosity, I came to learn of the Deutsches Institut für Normung headquartered in Berlin, and its beginnings (in 1922), when this German institution first published a methodology of assessing standards.
The A4 paper format attracted my attention to a functional object, the desk, which we make use of for different mental and physical forms of movement, like taking measurements, writing, thinking, cutting, erasing.

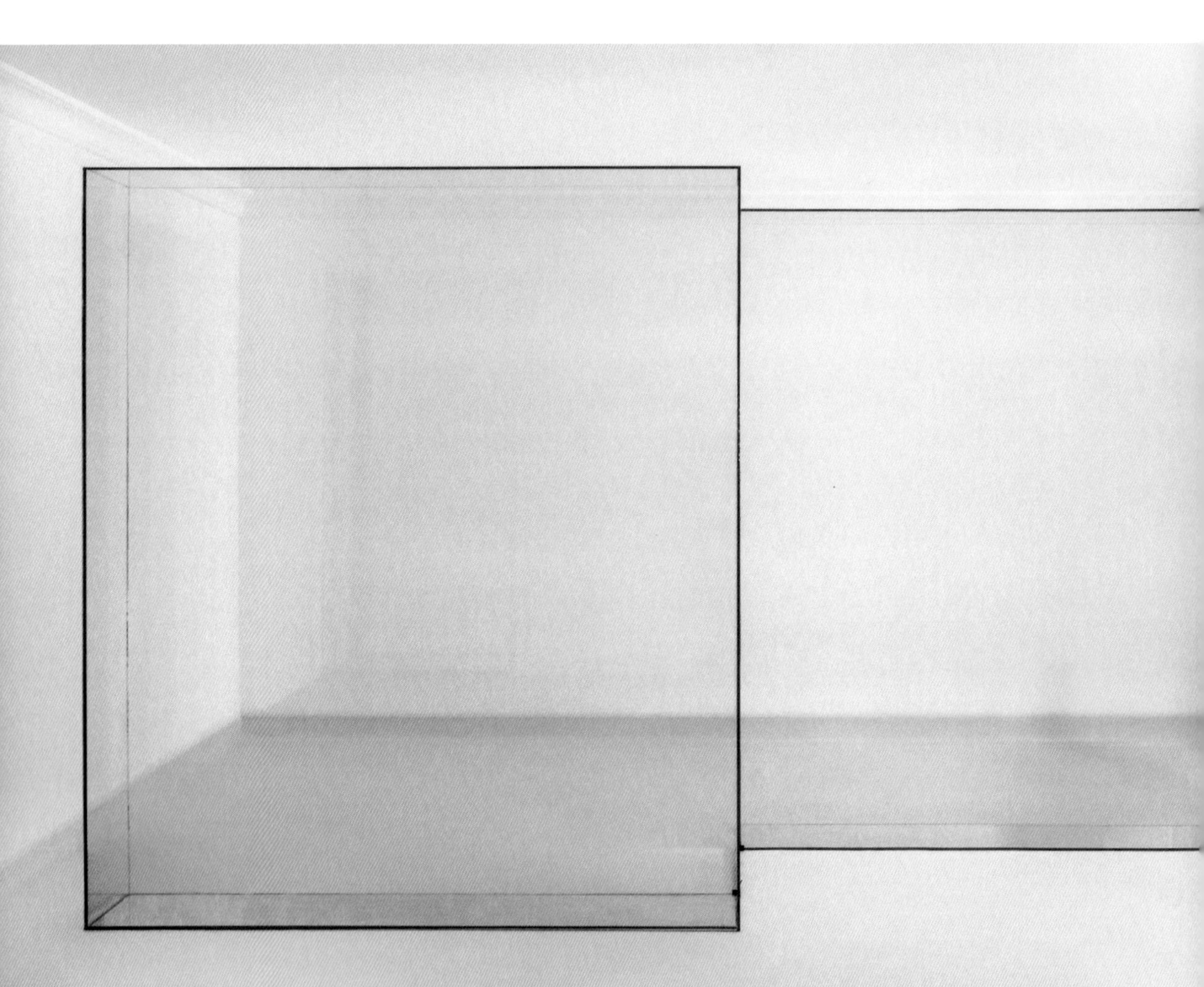

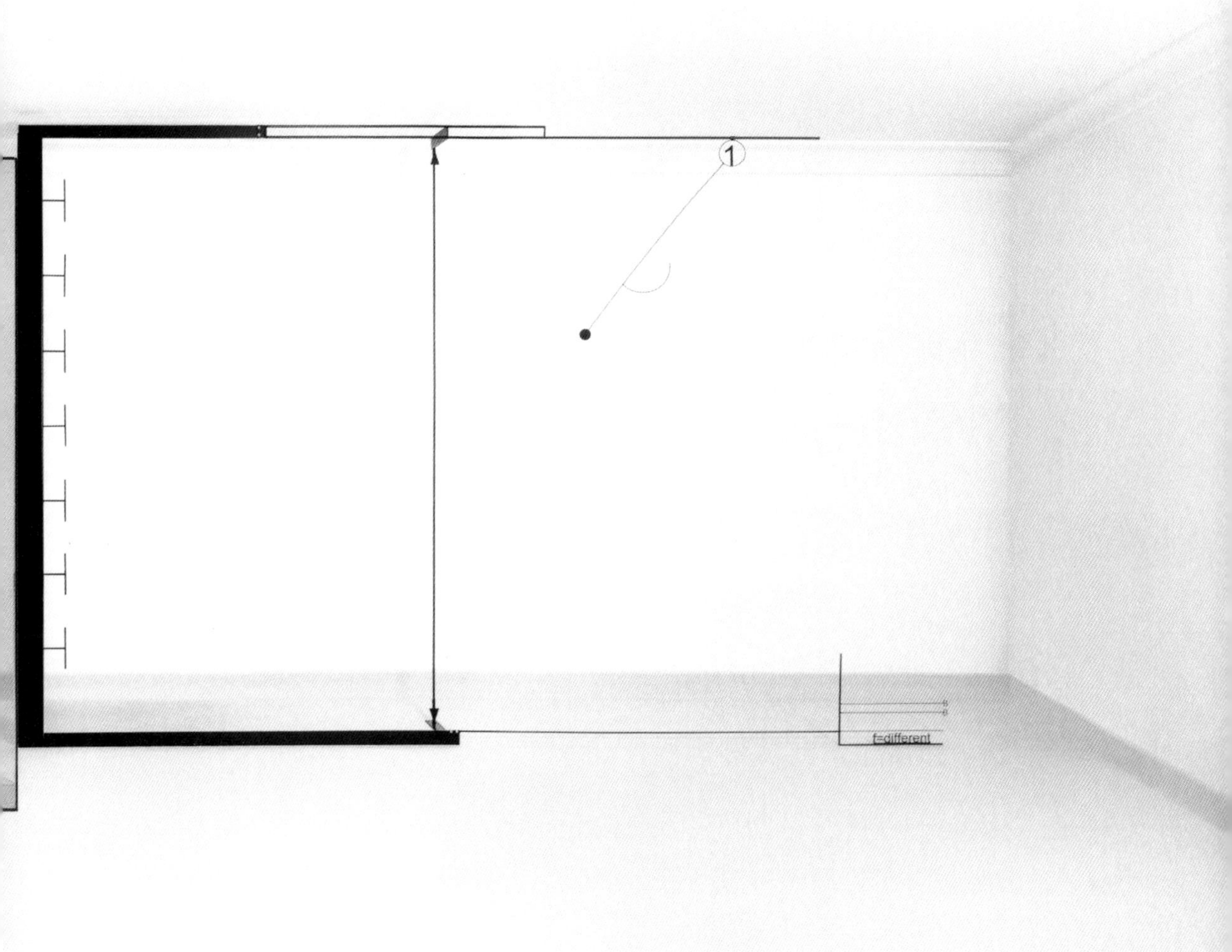
1
f=different

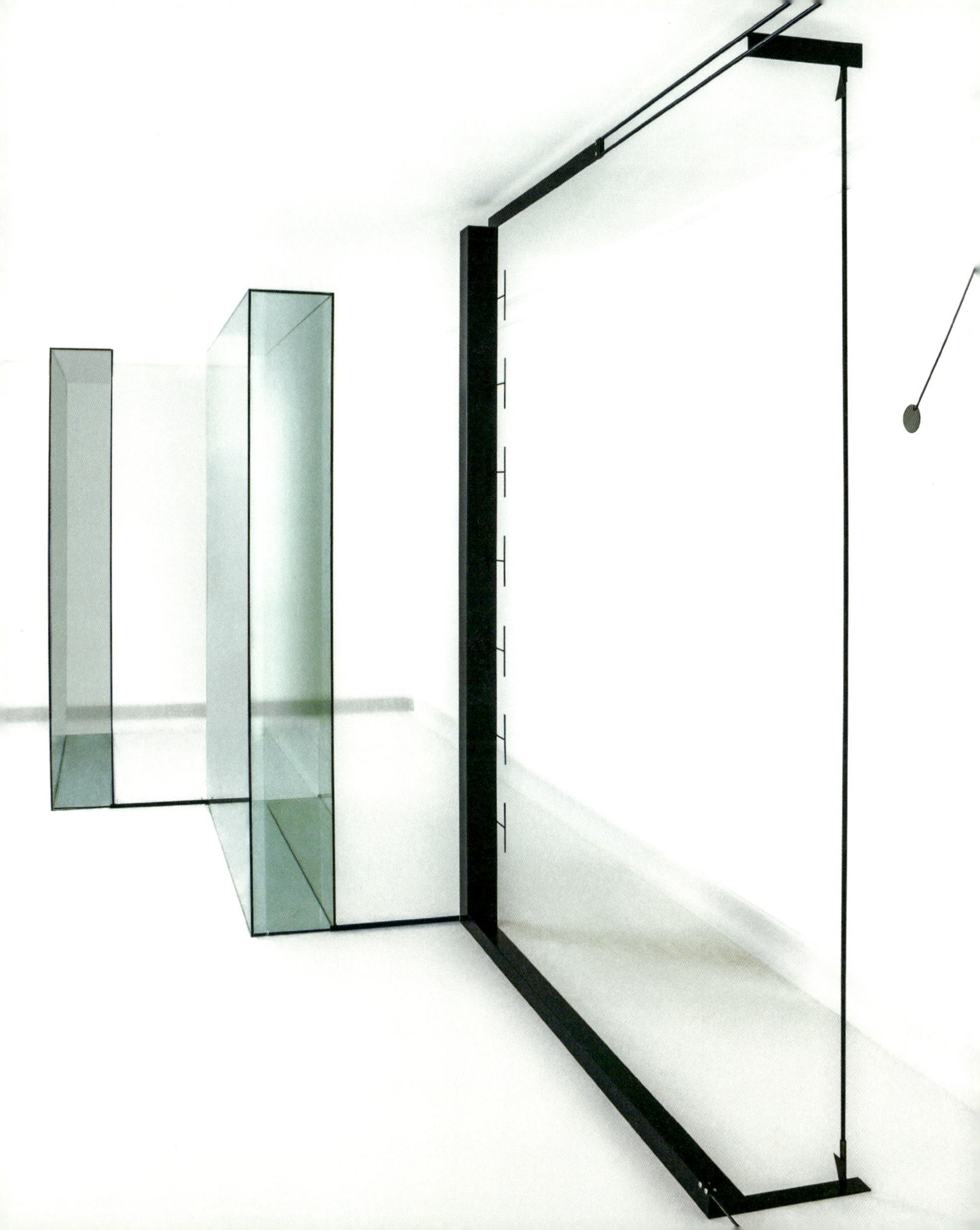

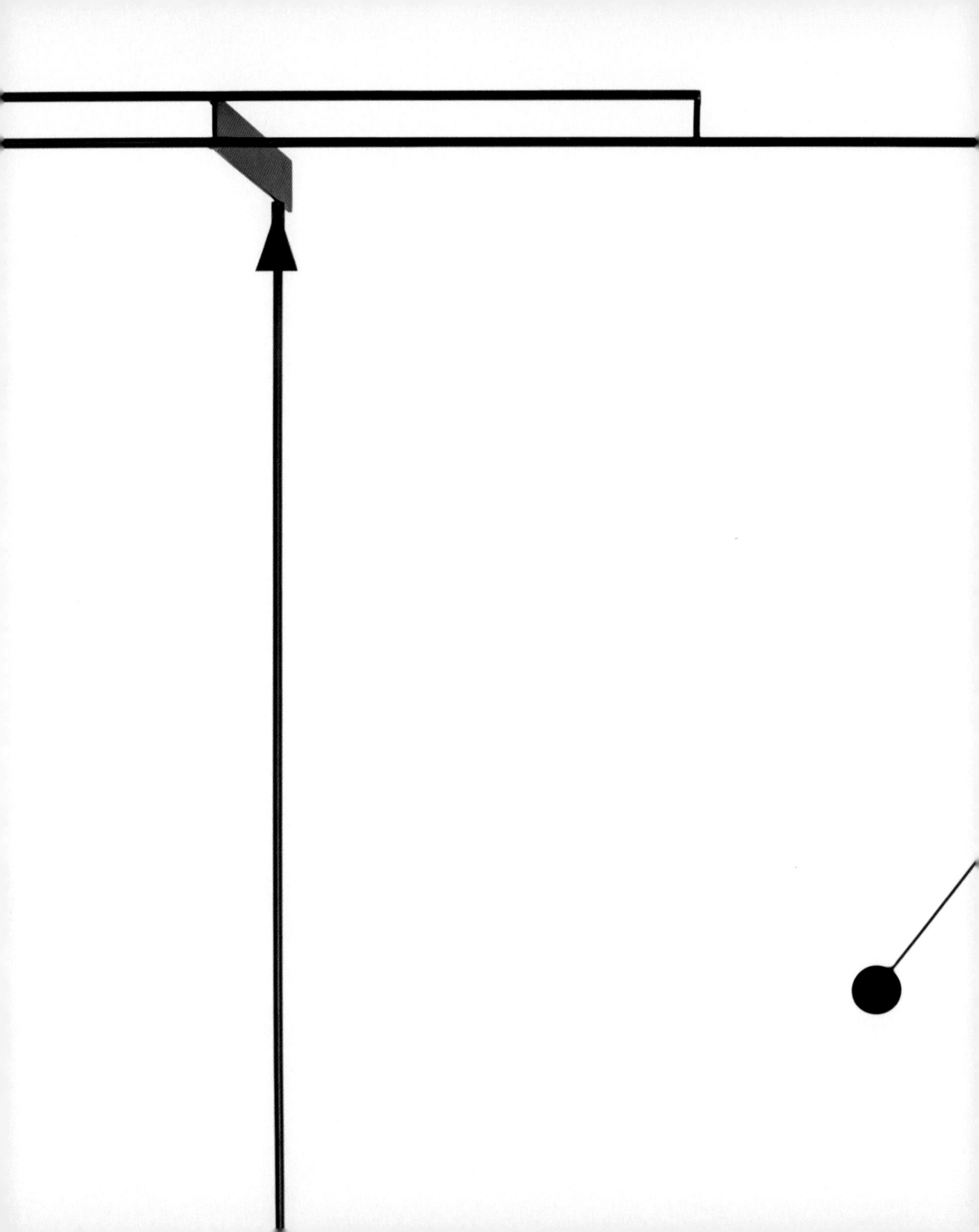

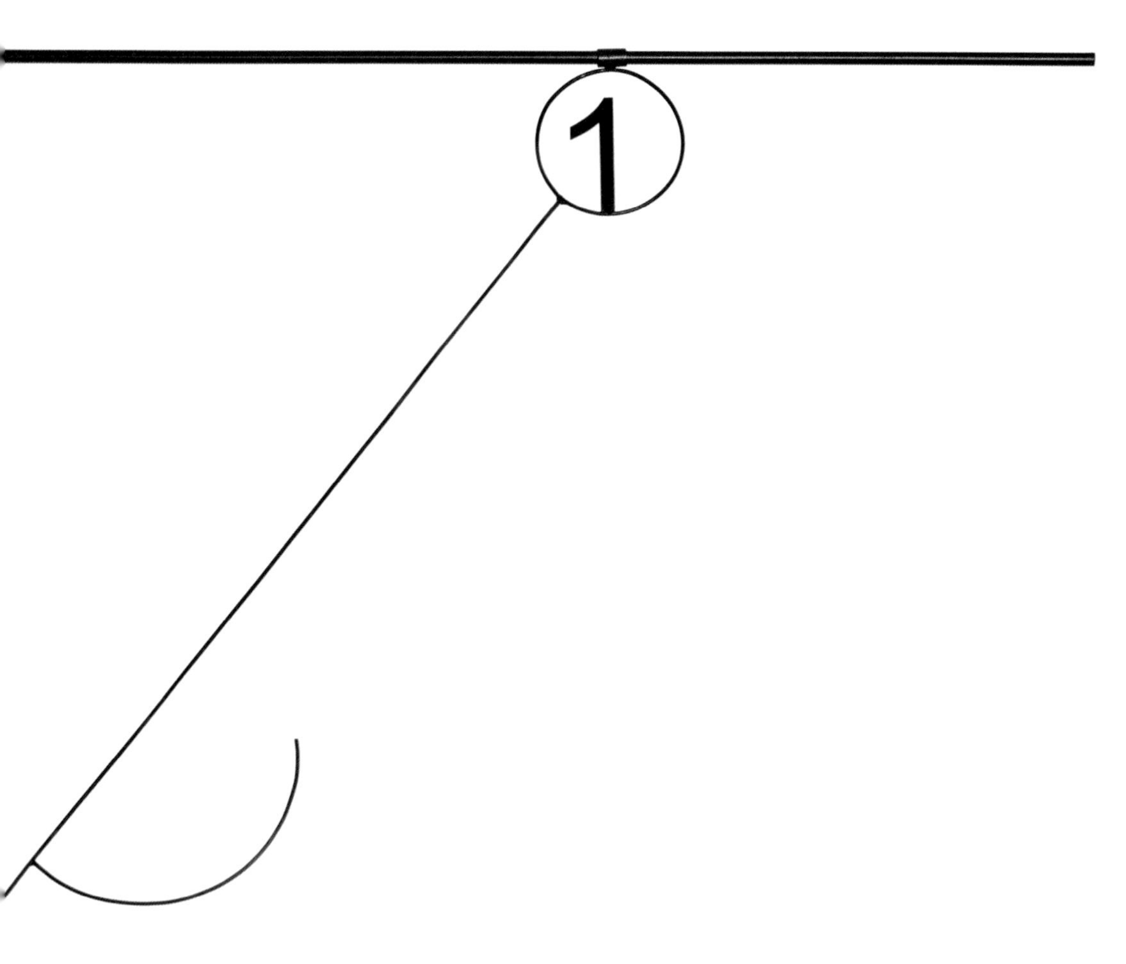
1

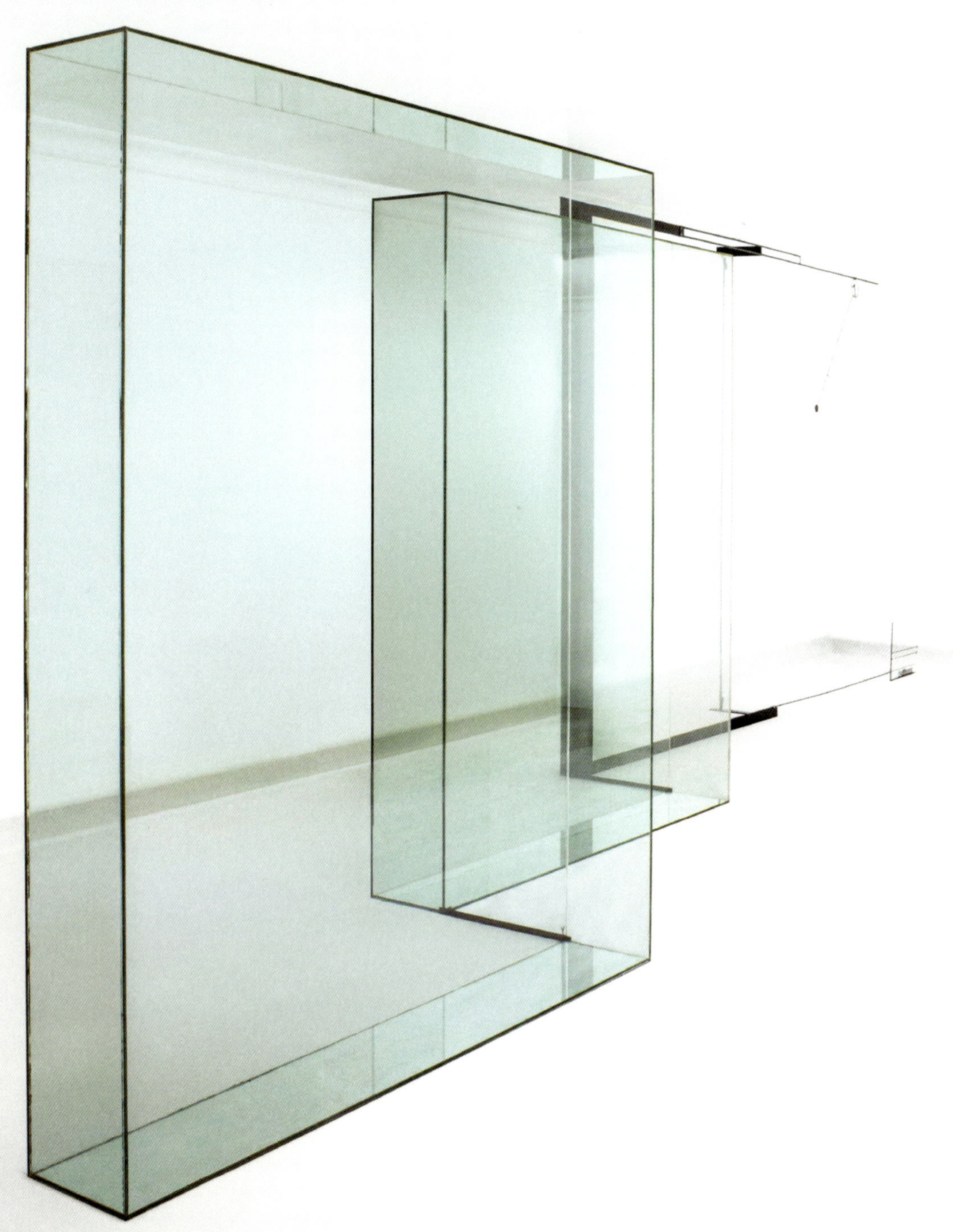

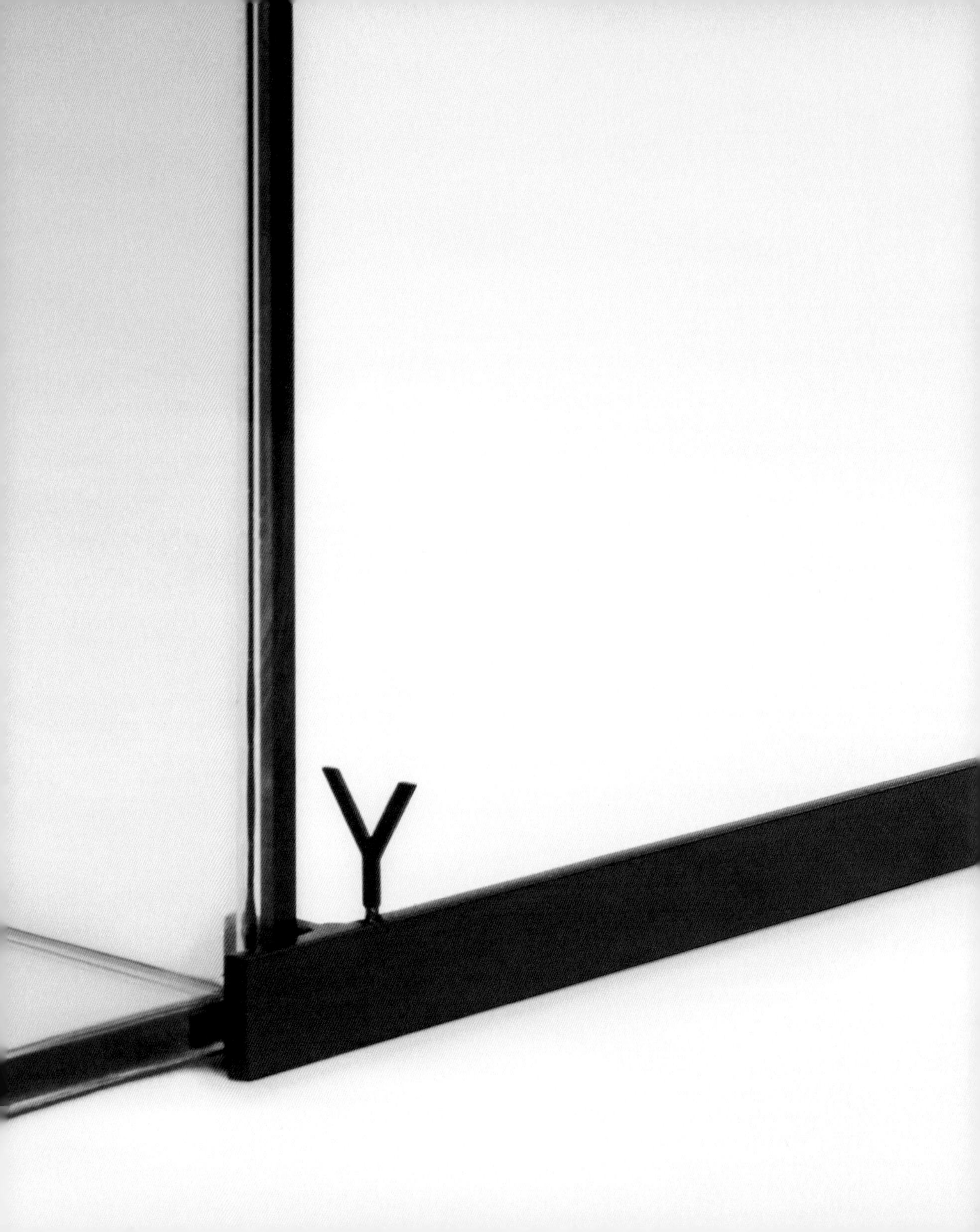
Y

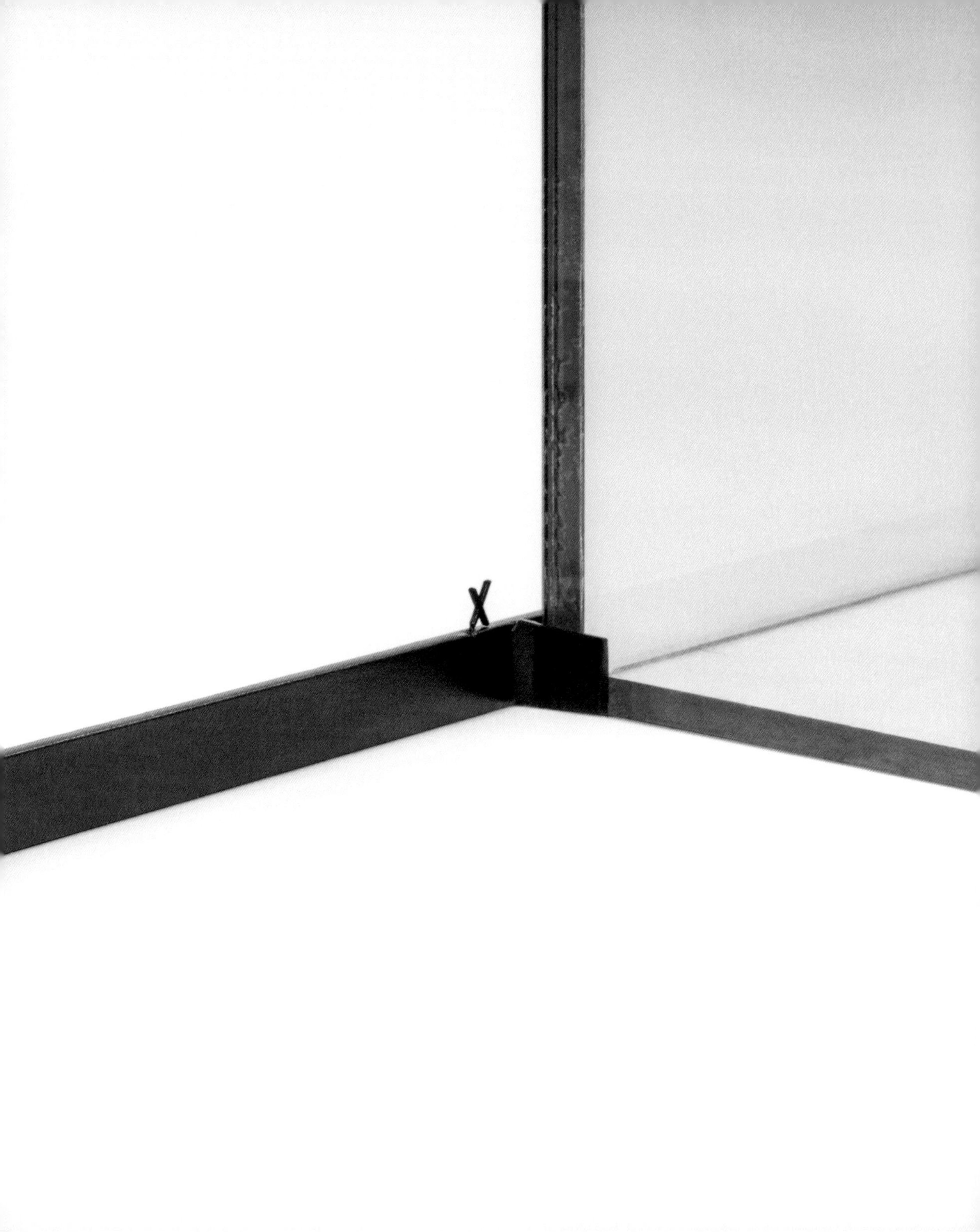

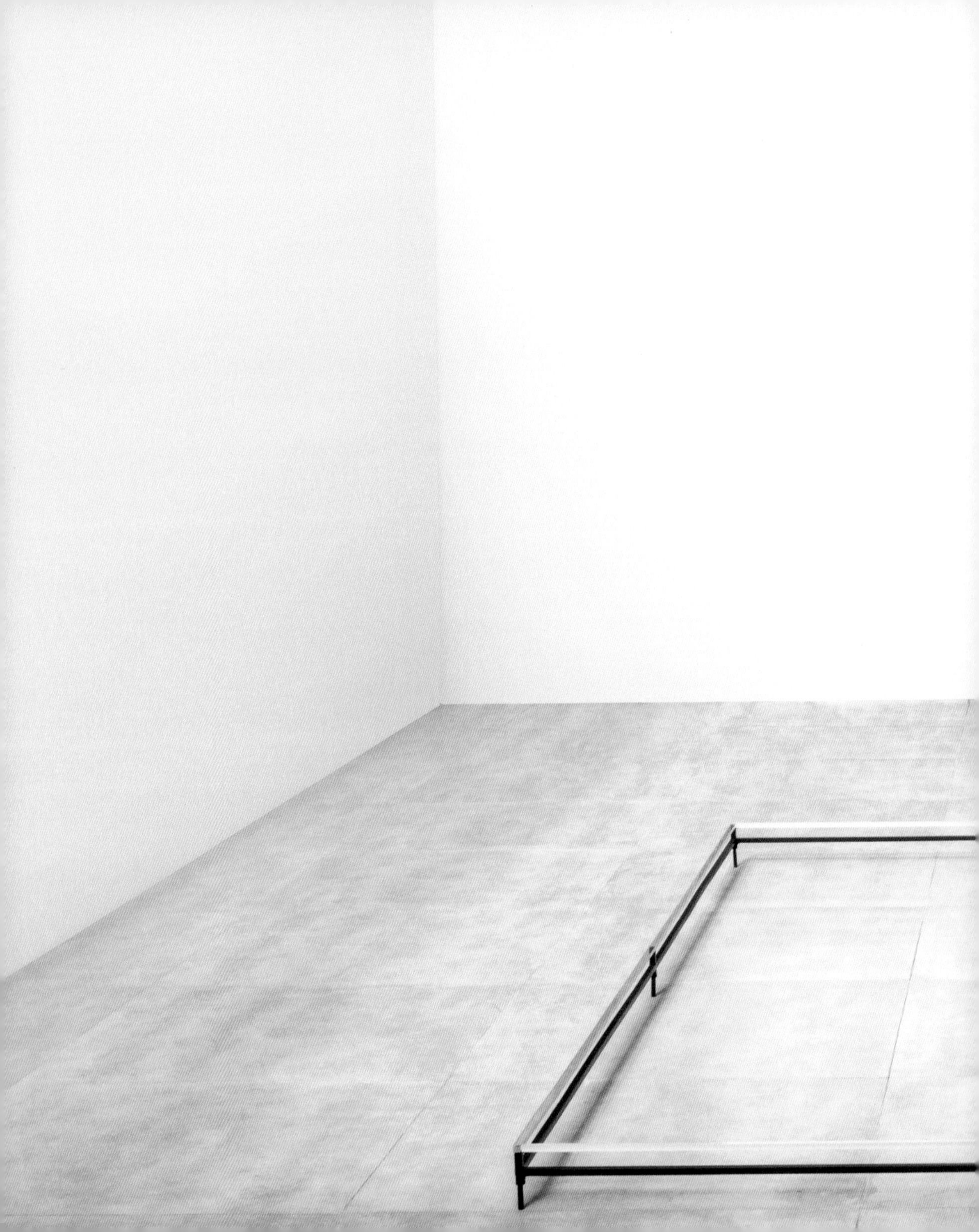

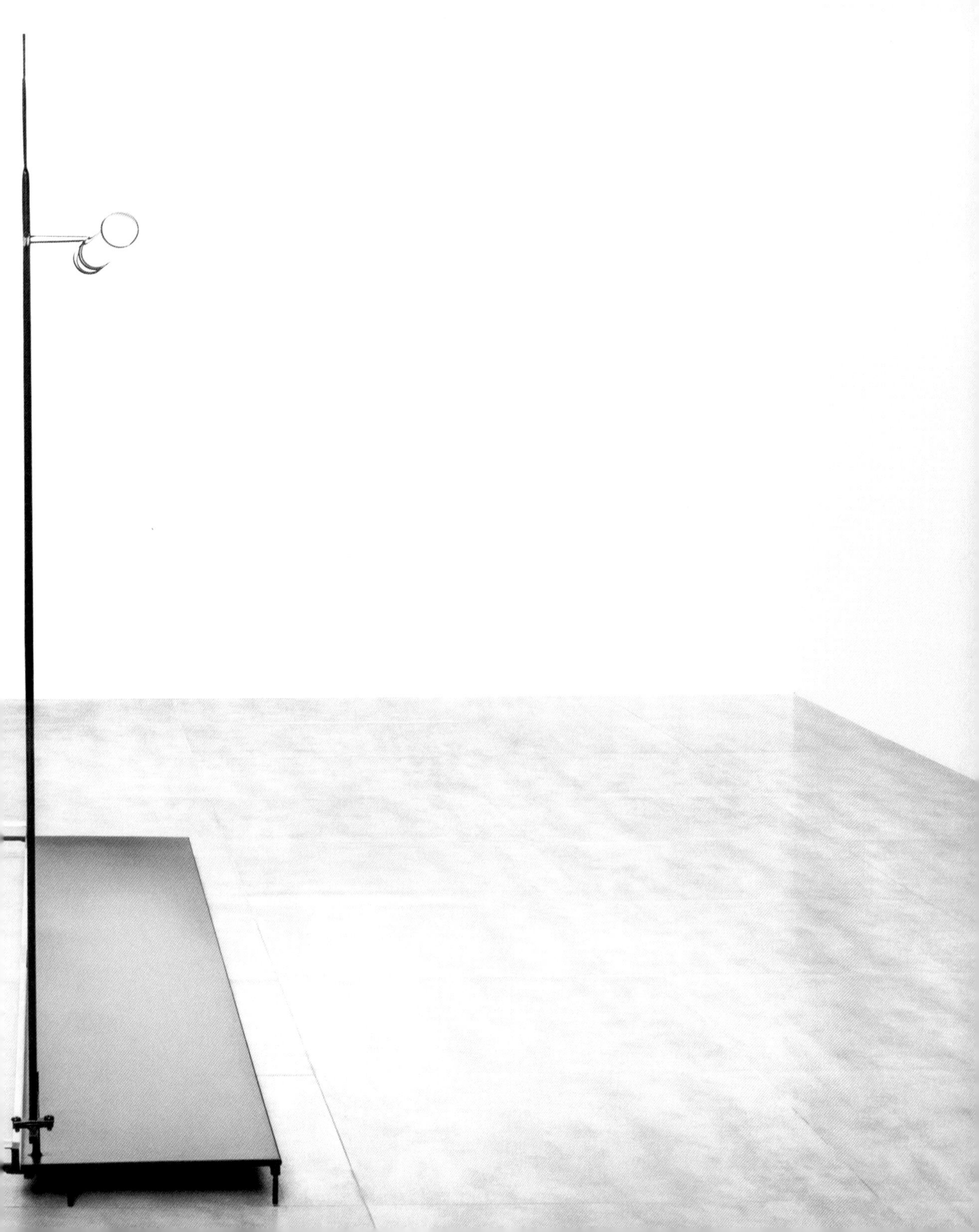

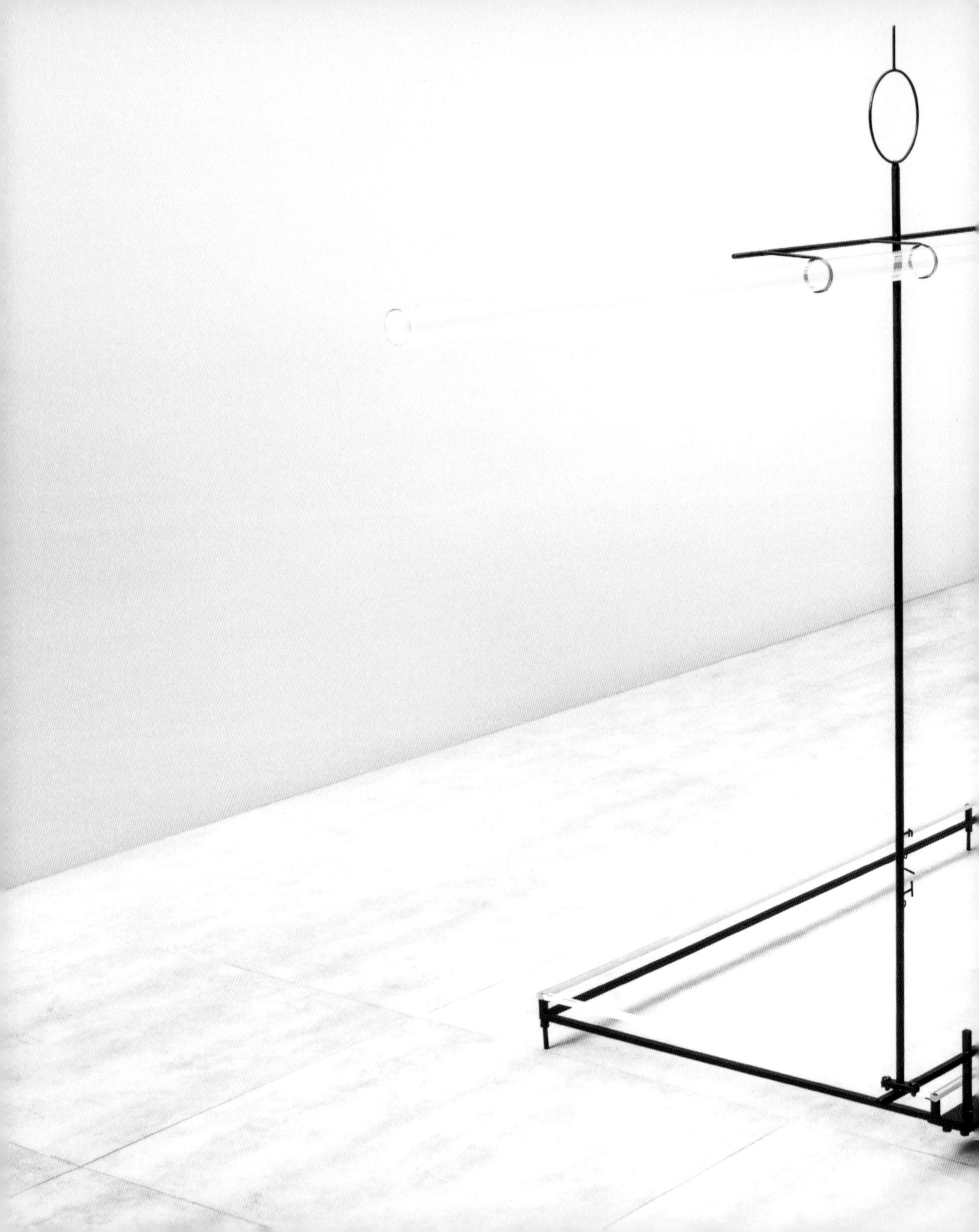

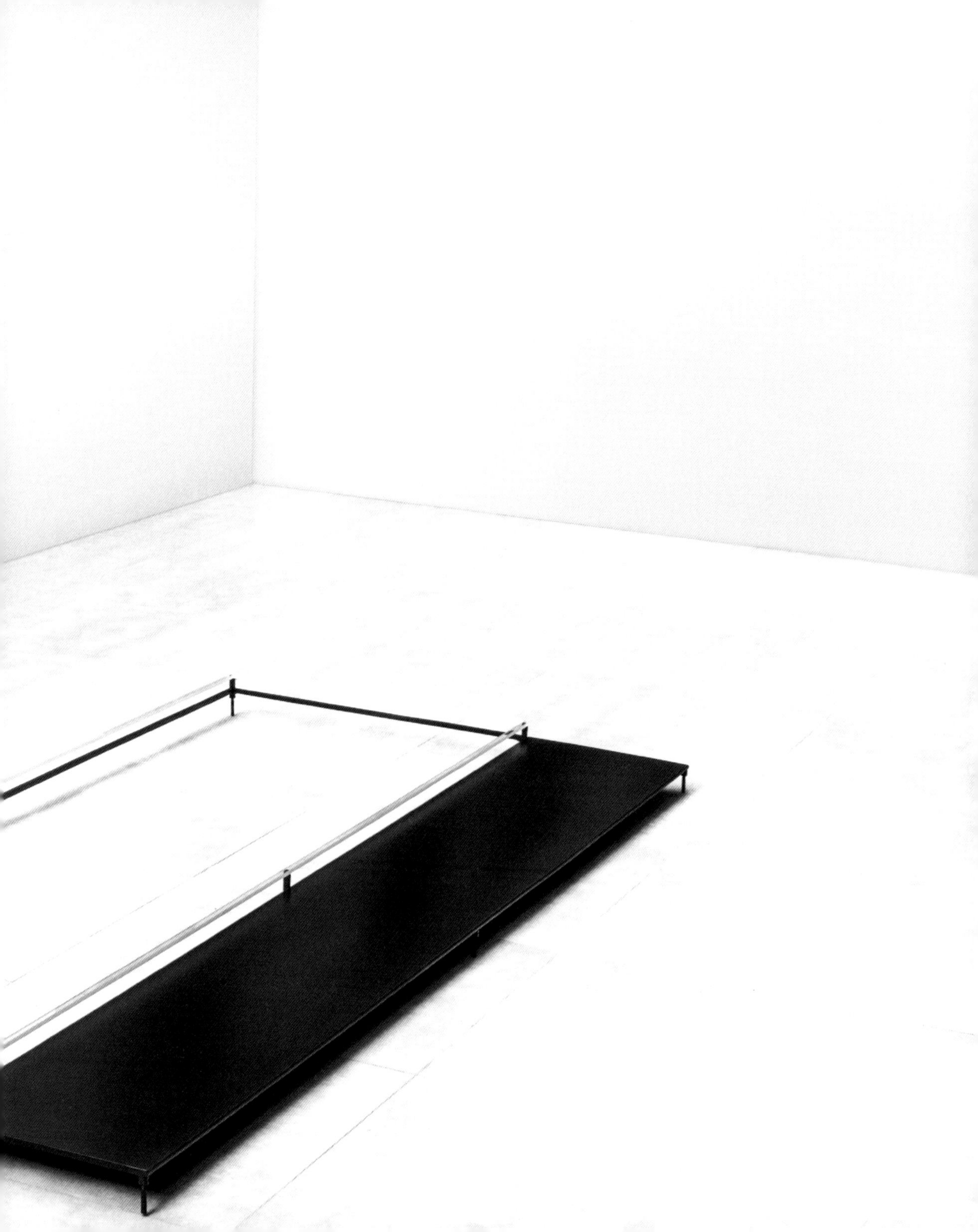

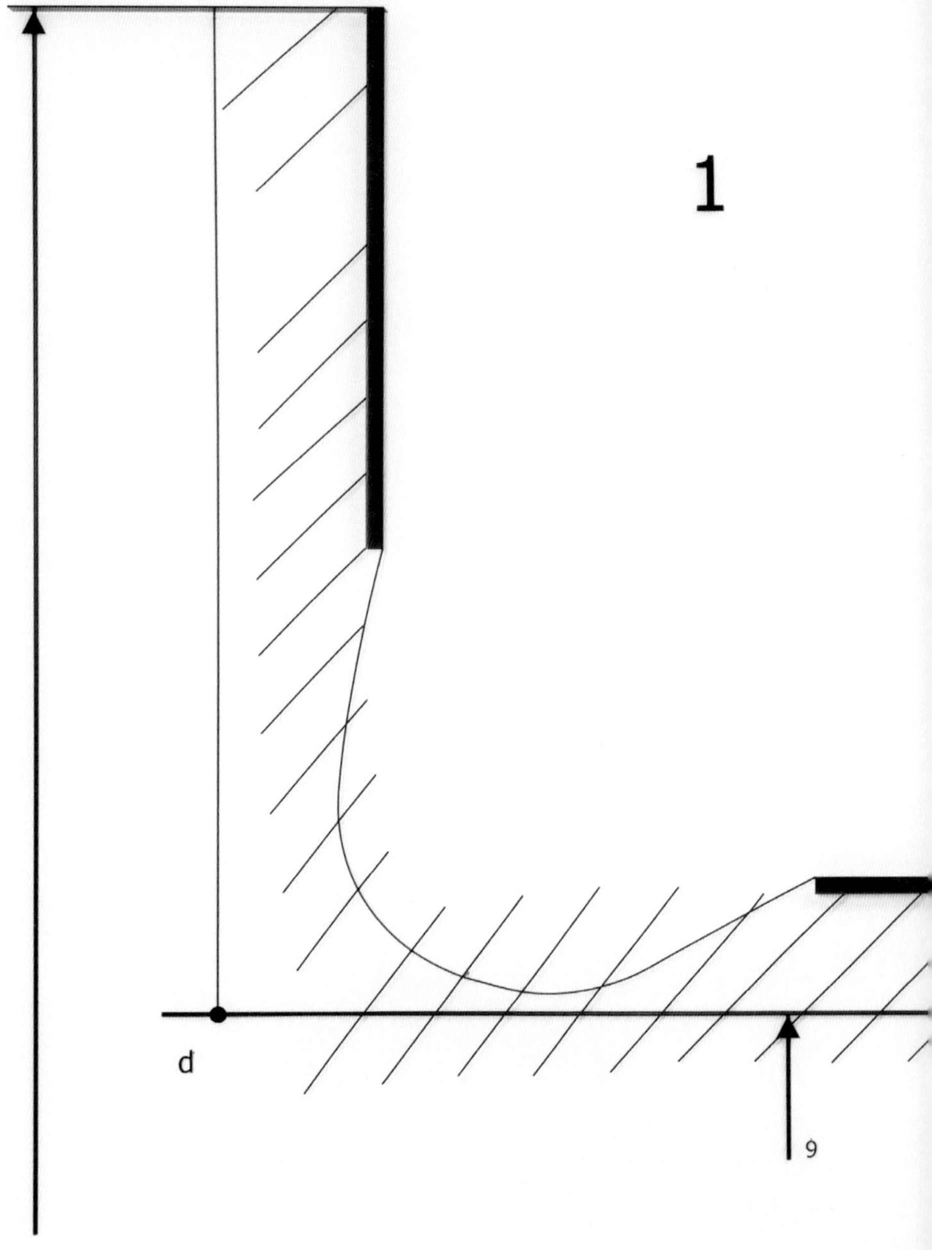

1
d
9

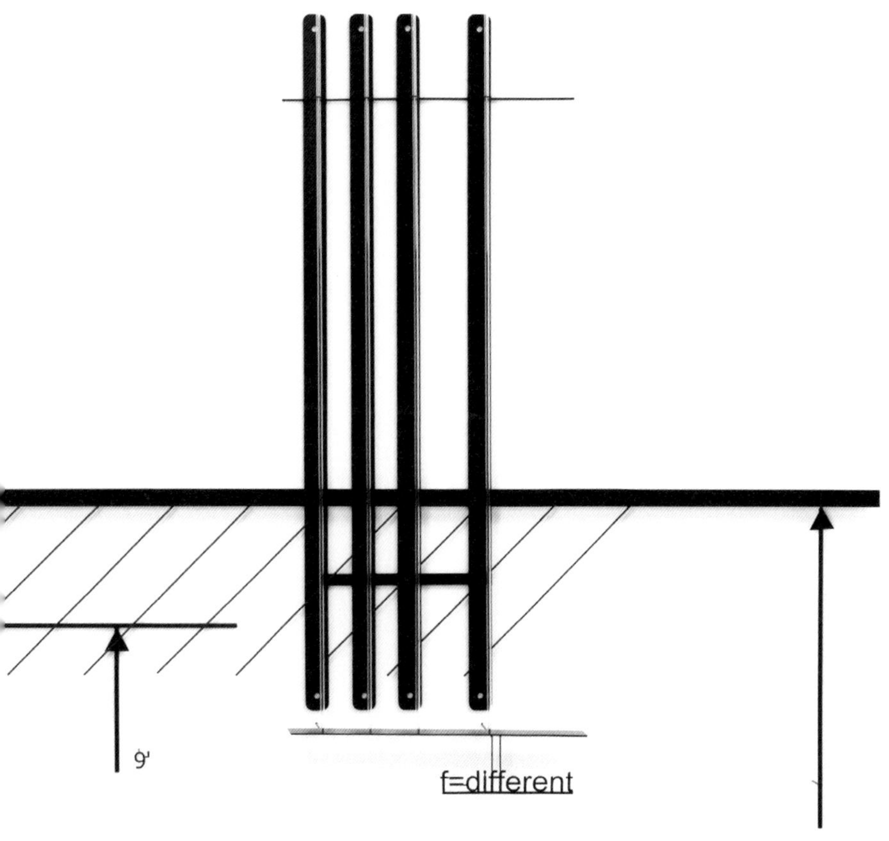

9'
f=different

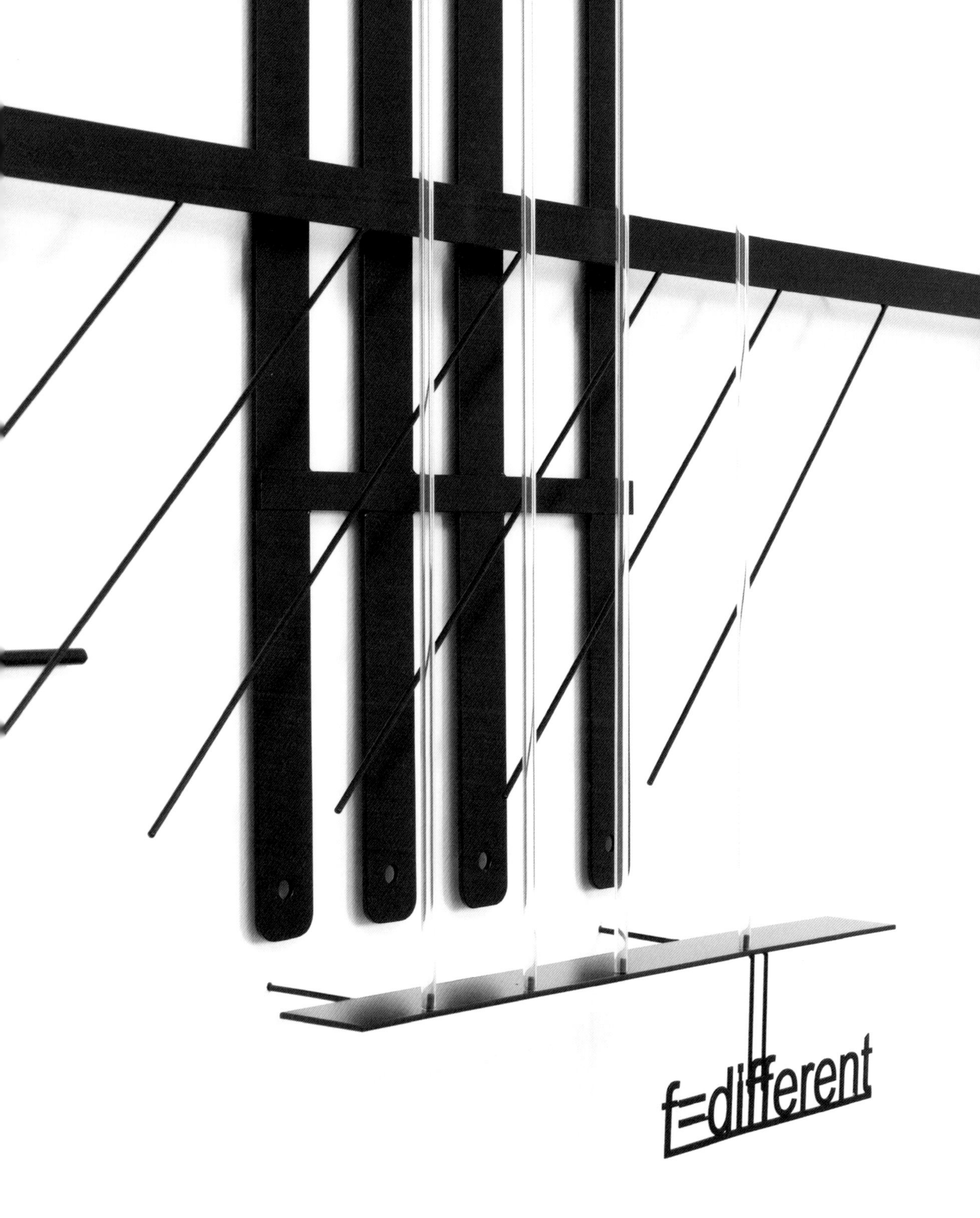
f=different

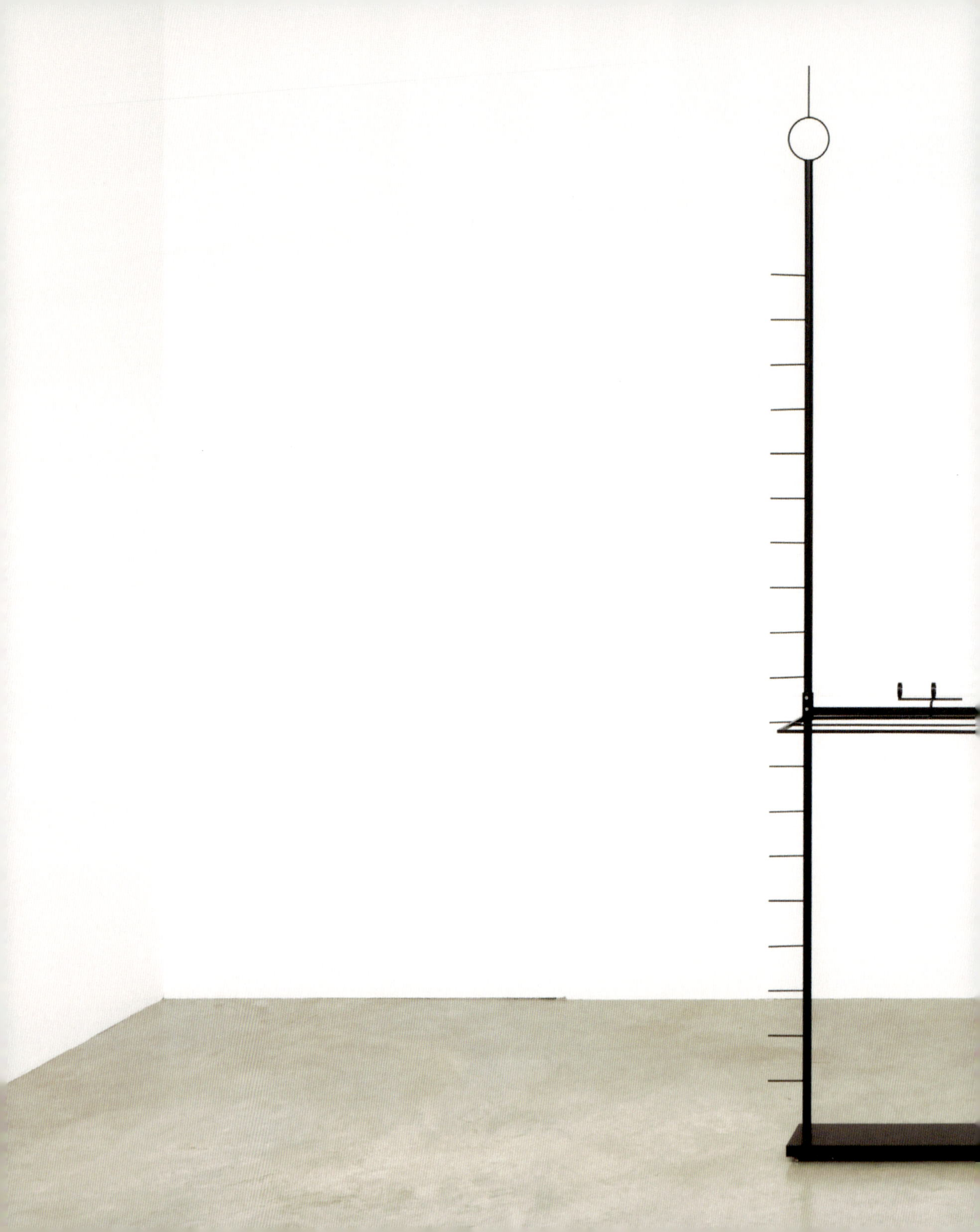

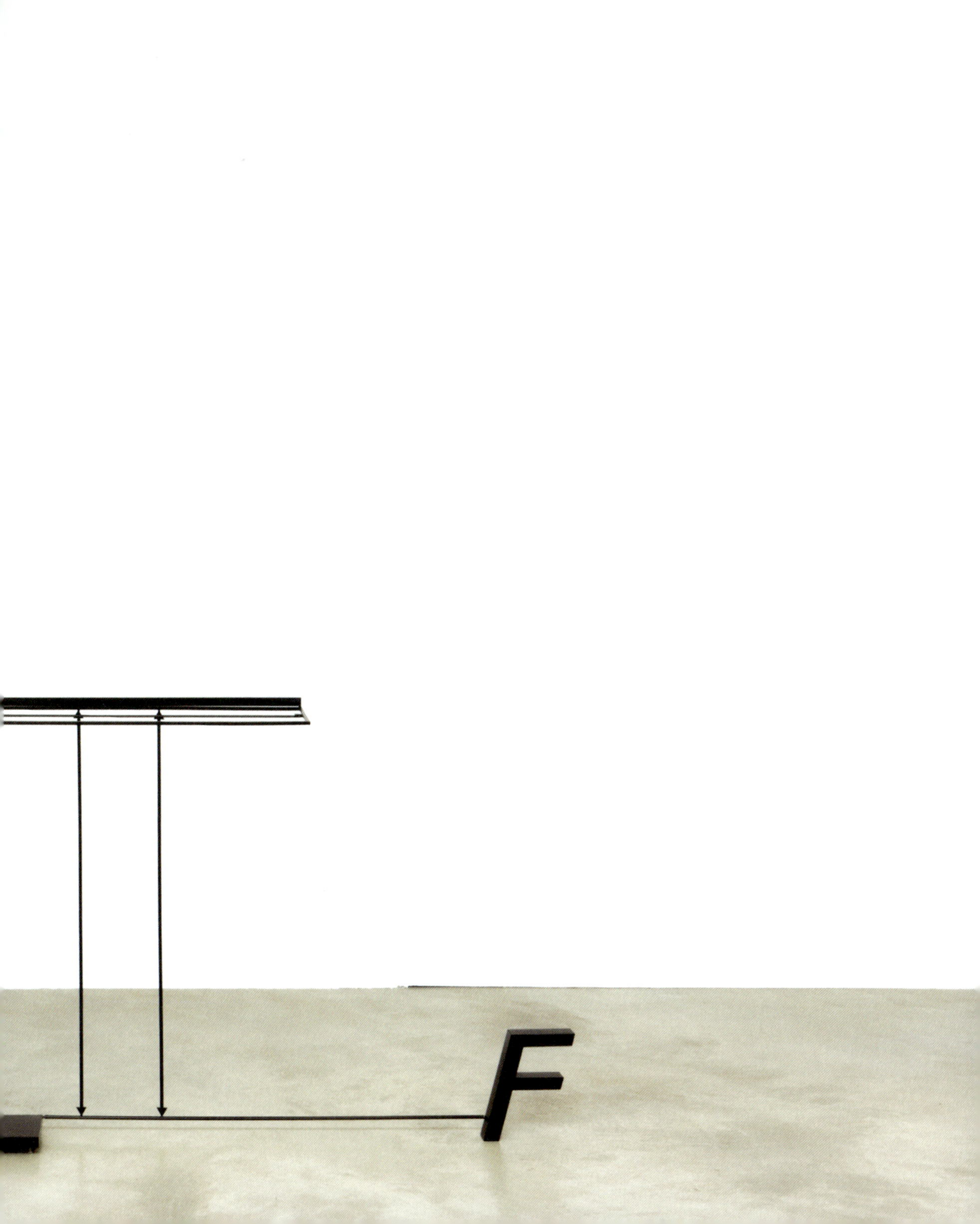

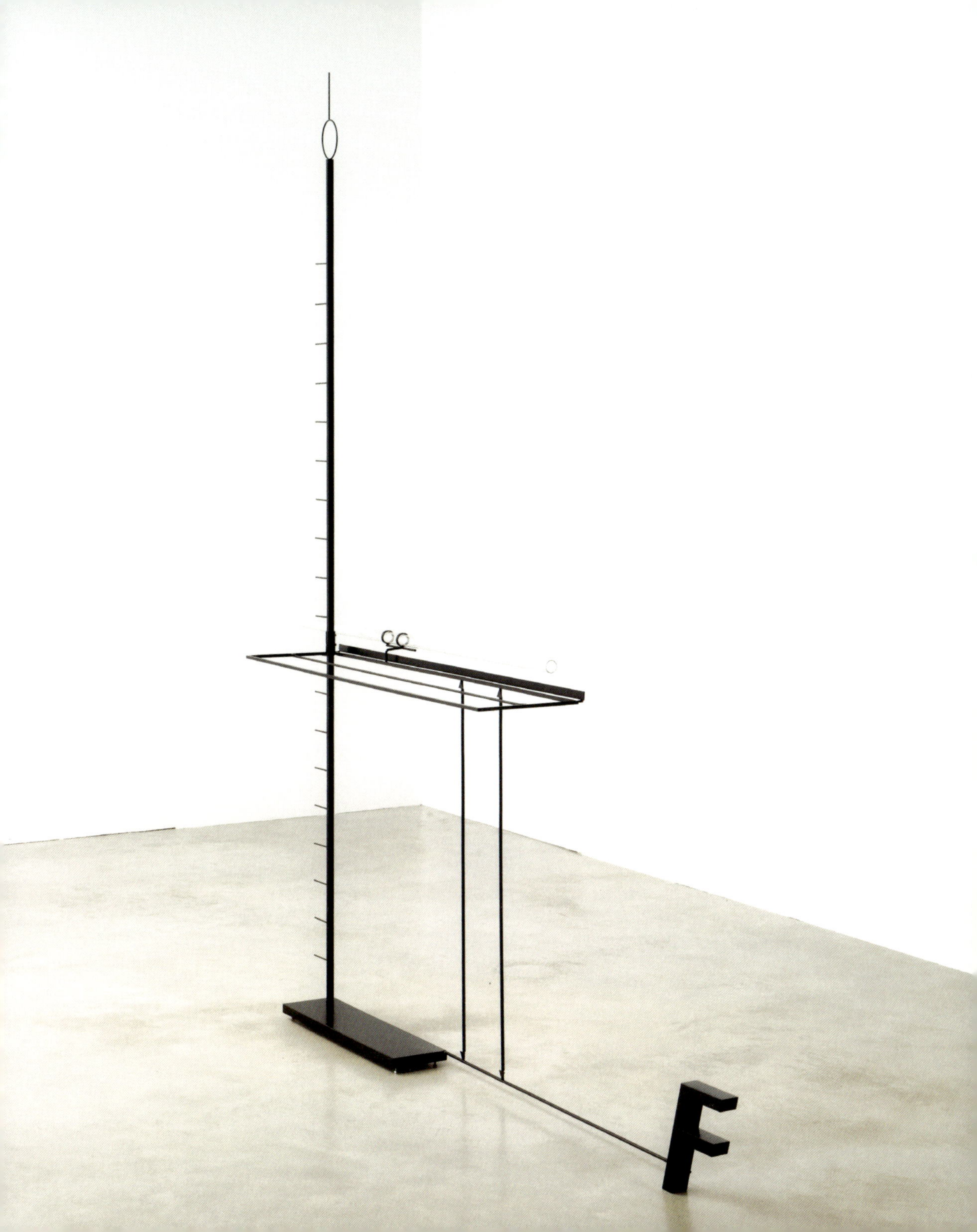

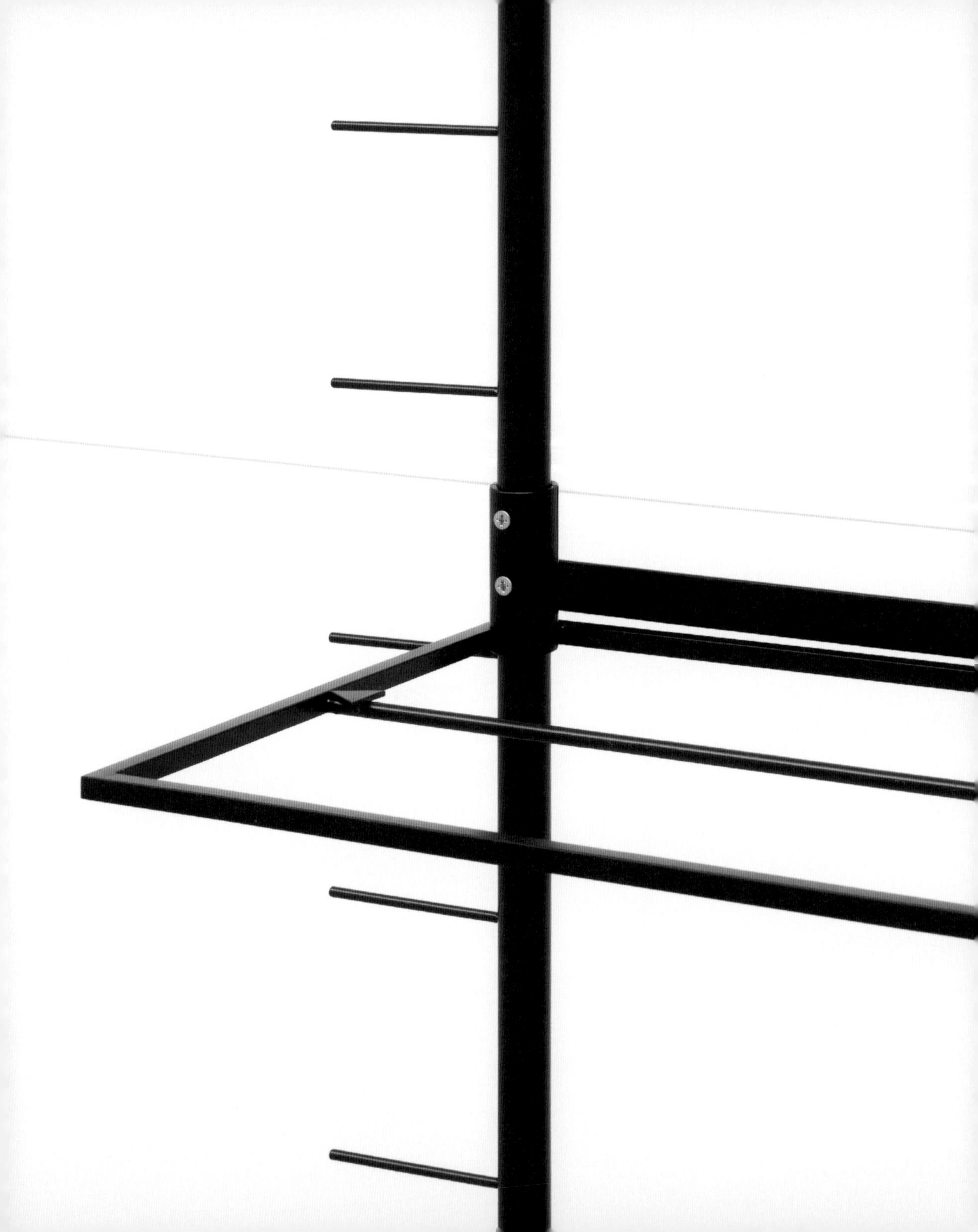

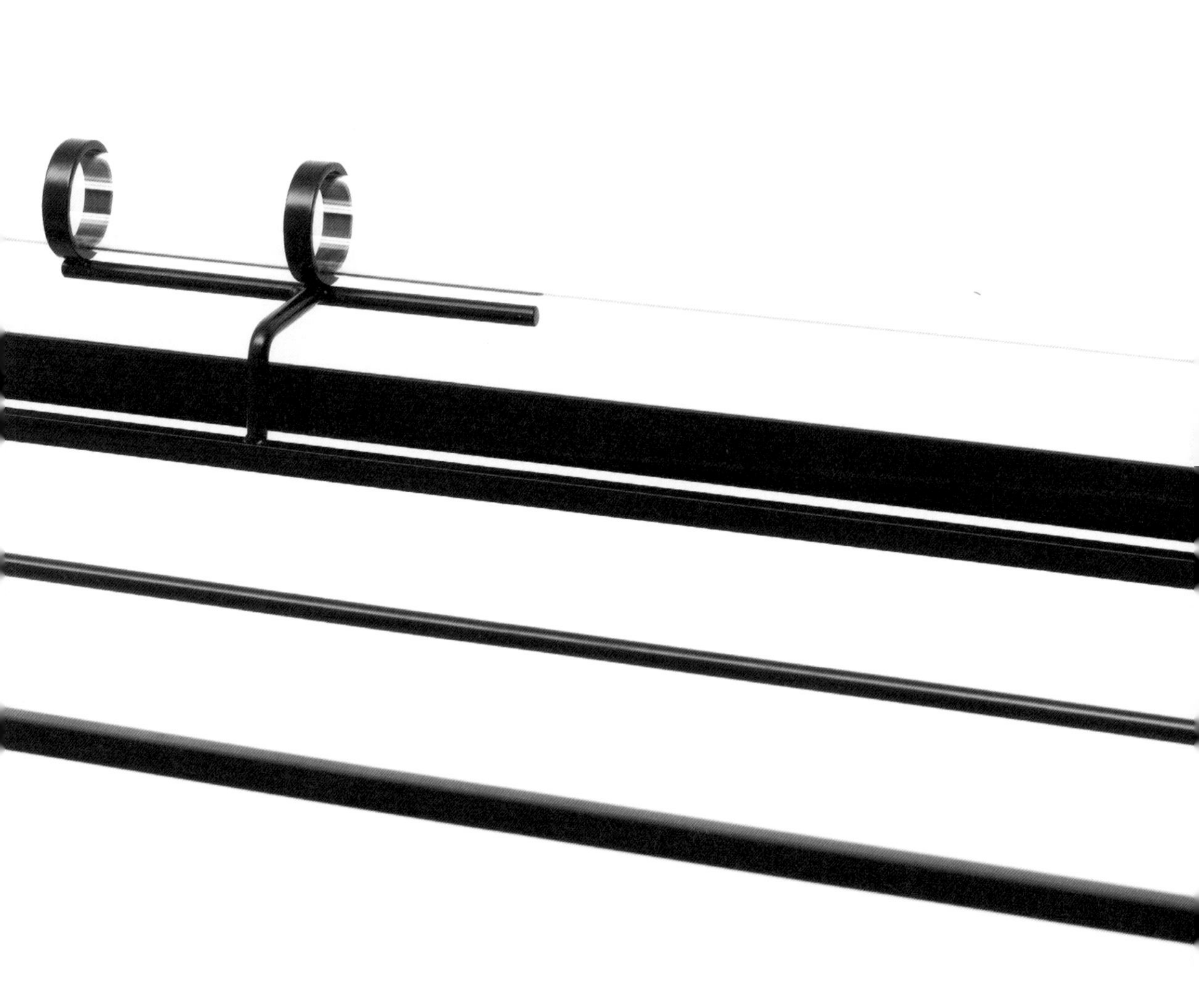

unprotected 0	unprotected 0	unprotected 0	unprotected 0
fig. 1	fig. 1	fig. 2	fig. 2
2015, sculpture powdercoated steel glass 280 x 130 x 26 cm	2015, collage print on paper steel, glass 21 x 29,7 cm	2015, sculpture powdercoated steel glass 240 x 320 x 142 cm	2015, collage print on paper steel, glass 21 x 29,7 cm

unprotected 0	unprotected 0
fig. 3	fig. 3
2015, sculpture powdercoated steel glass 262 x 58 x 36 cm	2015, collage print on paper steel, glass 21 x 29,7 cm

0

"unprotected 0" series

The idea of measurement is subject to uncertainty. A measured value is only complete if it is accompanied by a statement on its inherent uncertainty. This statement is crucial for the "unprotected 0" series, which focuses on the uncertainty of measurement. Composed of large free-standing sculptures made of black iron and glass coated with powder and a group of sculptural collages, this series centers on the theme of calibration in a larger sense. It reveals a language that can only be understood between the engineer and the technicians.

The series title "unprotected 0" is a reference to the value of system. It also addresses our position within the system. In working with language, I observe that letters and numbers are not innocent. They represent a certain class and a certain interest. Concepts of value and elimination are associated with this creating errors and a percentage of doubt. The title "unprotected 0" corresponds with the moment in which no assumptions can be made any more and with the idea that every shape has its own origin.

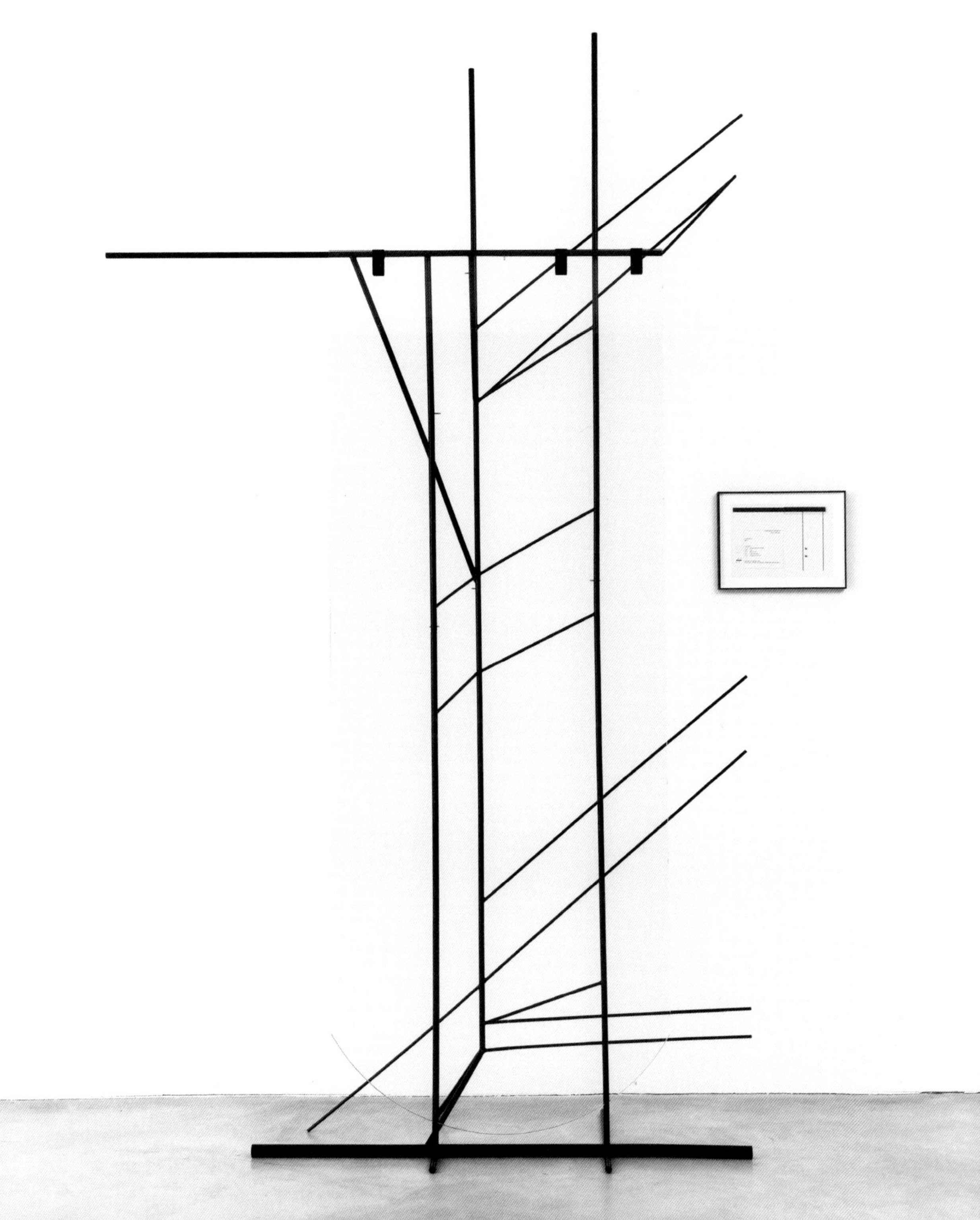

composition of mechanism
each compound

unprotected 0
fig. 1

ingredients :

7,3 % measurement uncertainty
0,3% error
0,4% edge of form
4,5% angle refraction
3,8% resistance of forces

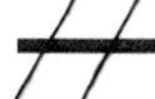

standard of shape accuracy
each value consists of at least four independent measurements

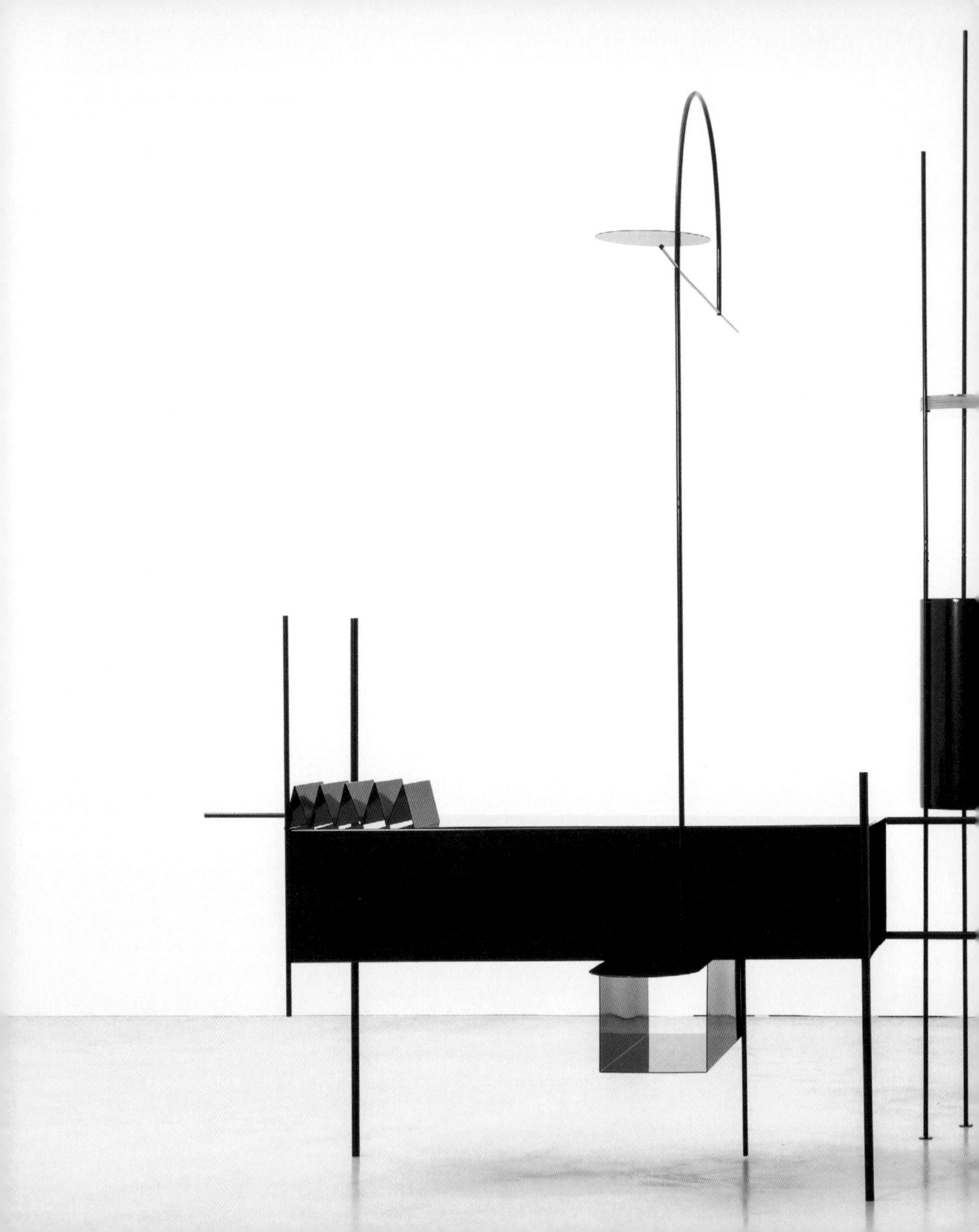

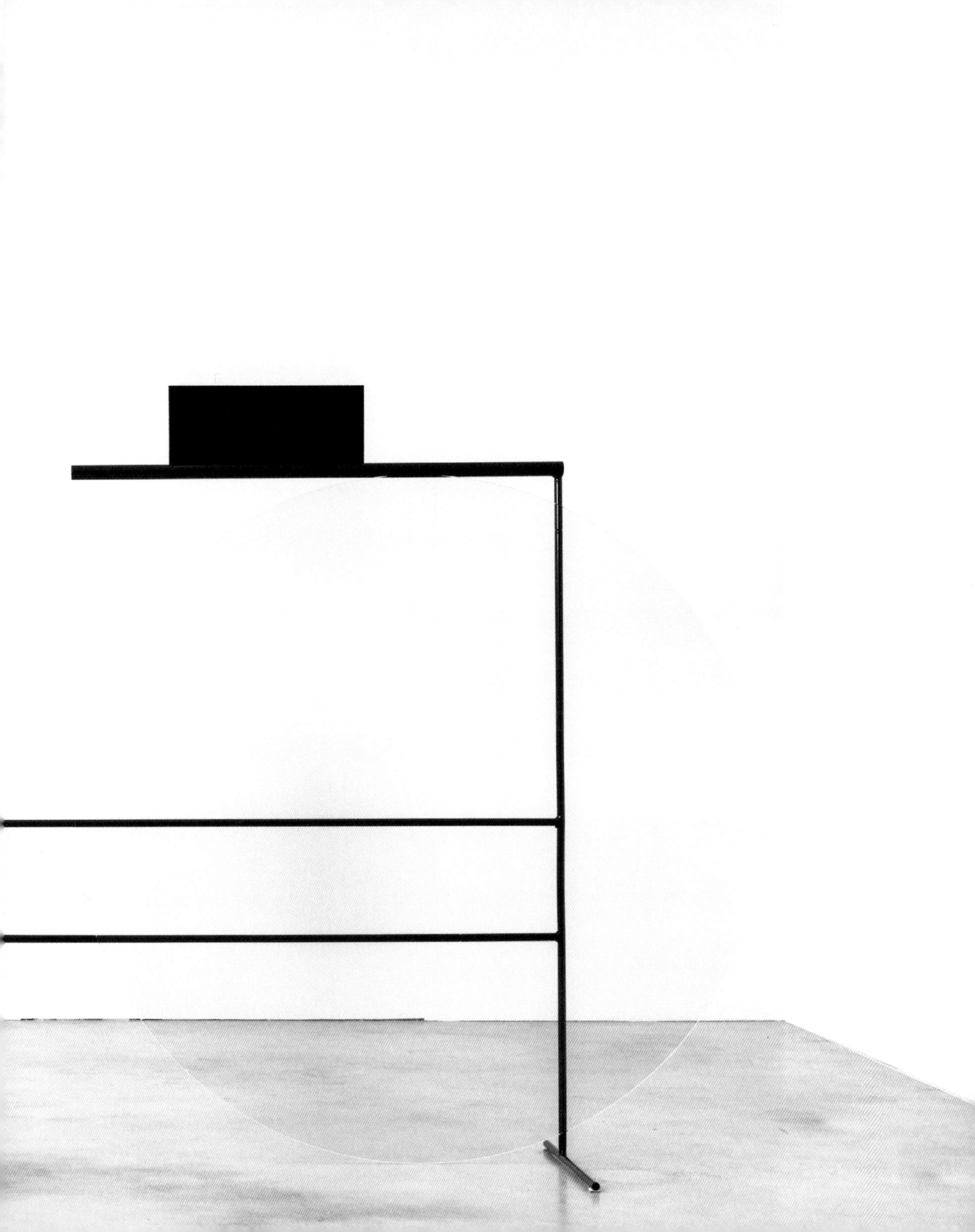

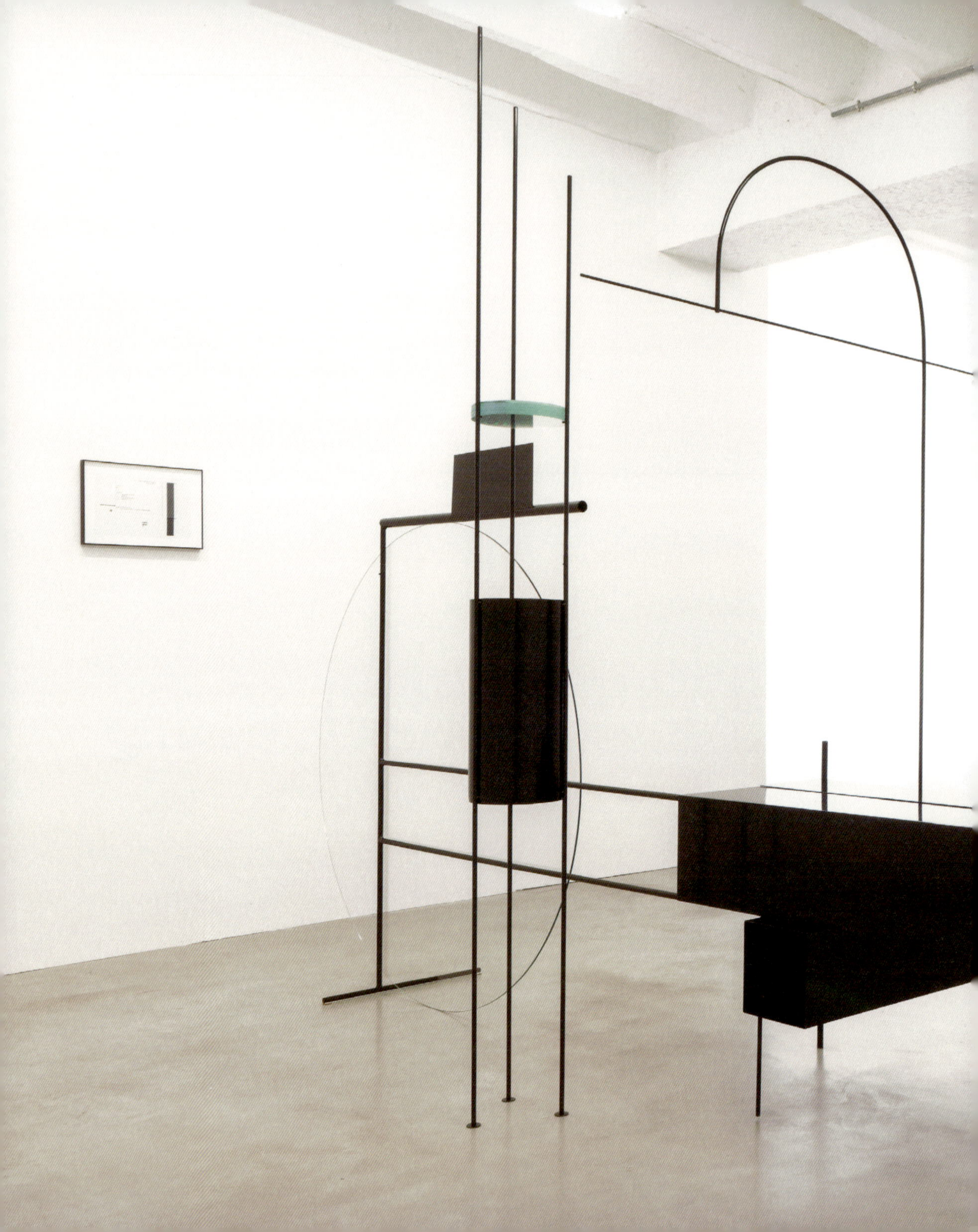

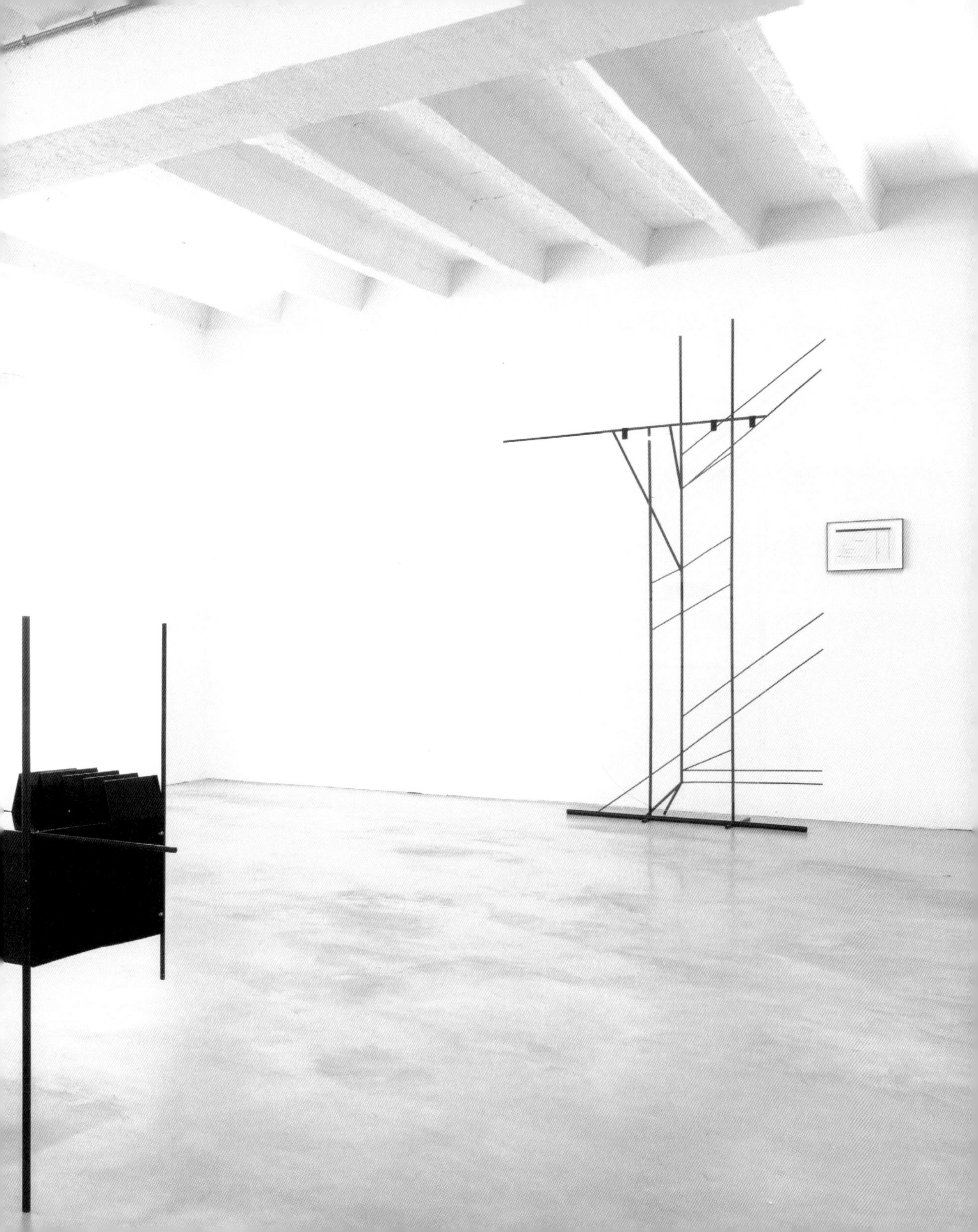

index of calibrated parameters
each instrument

unprotected 0

fig. 2

ingredients :

0,7% measurement uncertainty
0,3% random error
2,1 % dimensionless quantity
0,2 % confidence interval

standard of shape accuracy
each value consists of at least four independent measurements

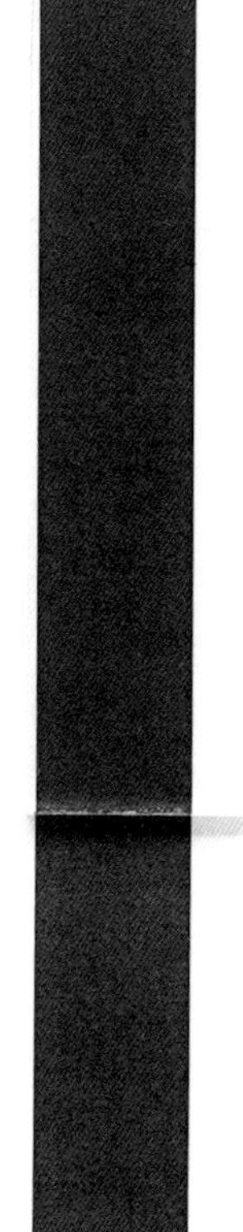

≠

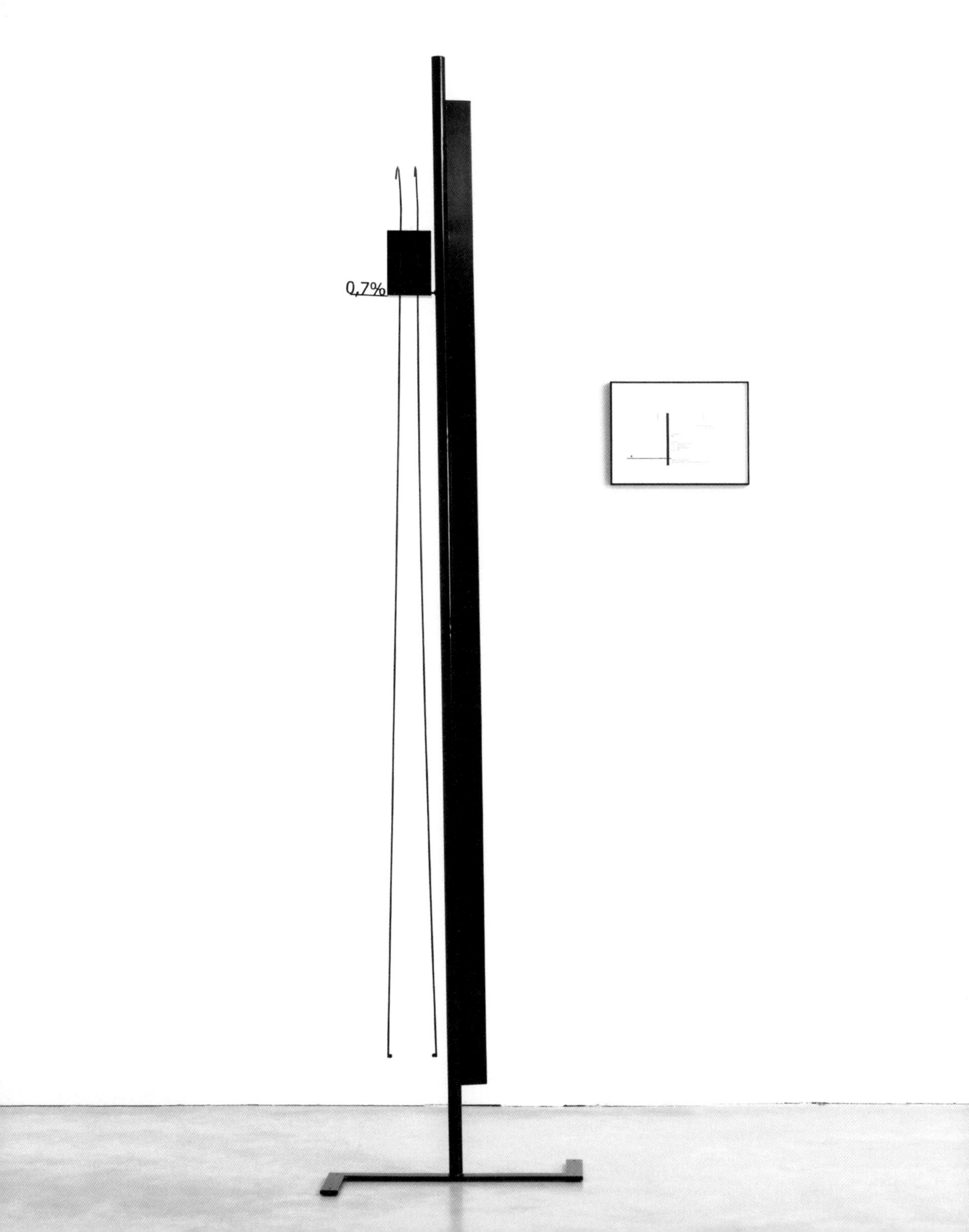
0,7%

structure of shape development
each instrument
unprotected 0
fig. 3

ingredients :
0,5% measurement uncertainty
1,2% point estimate
0,1 % edge line deflection
0,2% doubt
standard of shape accuracy
each value consists of at least four independent measurements

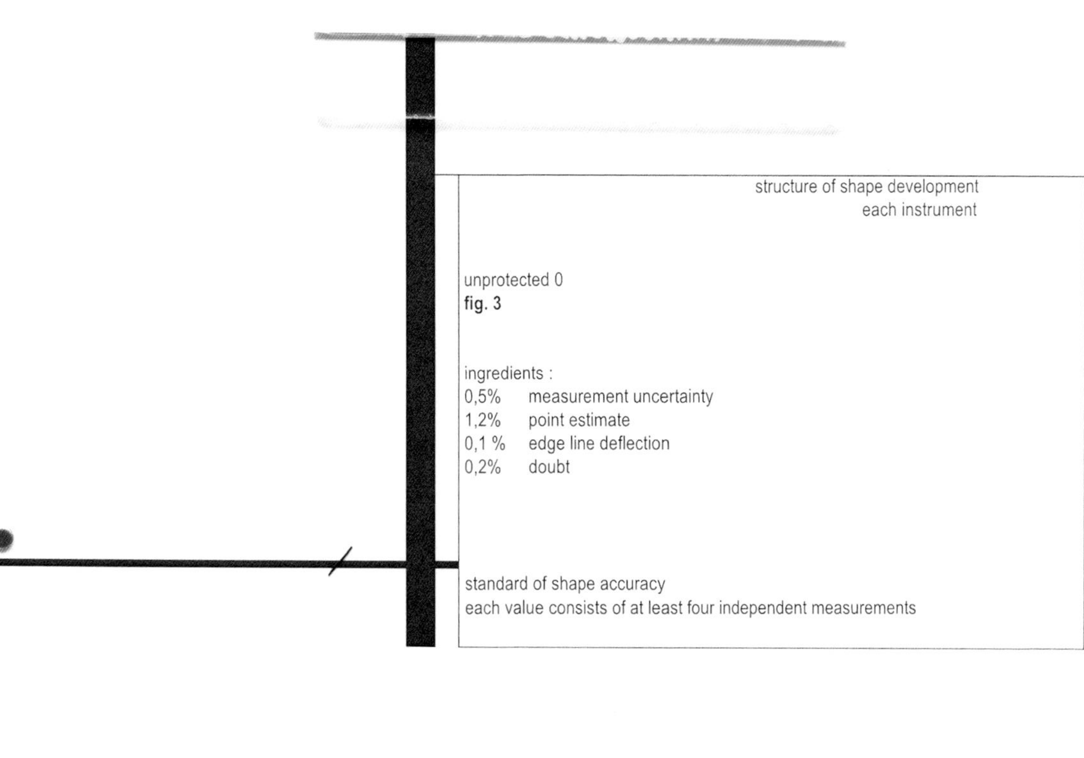

unprotected 0	unprotected 0	unprotected 0	unprotected 0
fig. 120°	fig. 120°	fig. 180°	fig. 180°
2015, sculpture powdercoated steel glass 240 x 177 x 137 cm	2015, collage print on paper steel 21 x 29,7 cm	2015, sculpture powdercoated steel glass 236 x 330 x 20 cm	2015, collage print on paper steel 21 x 29,7 cm

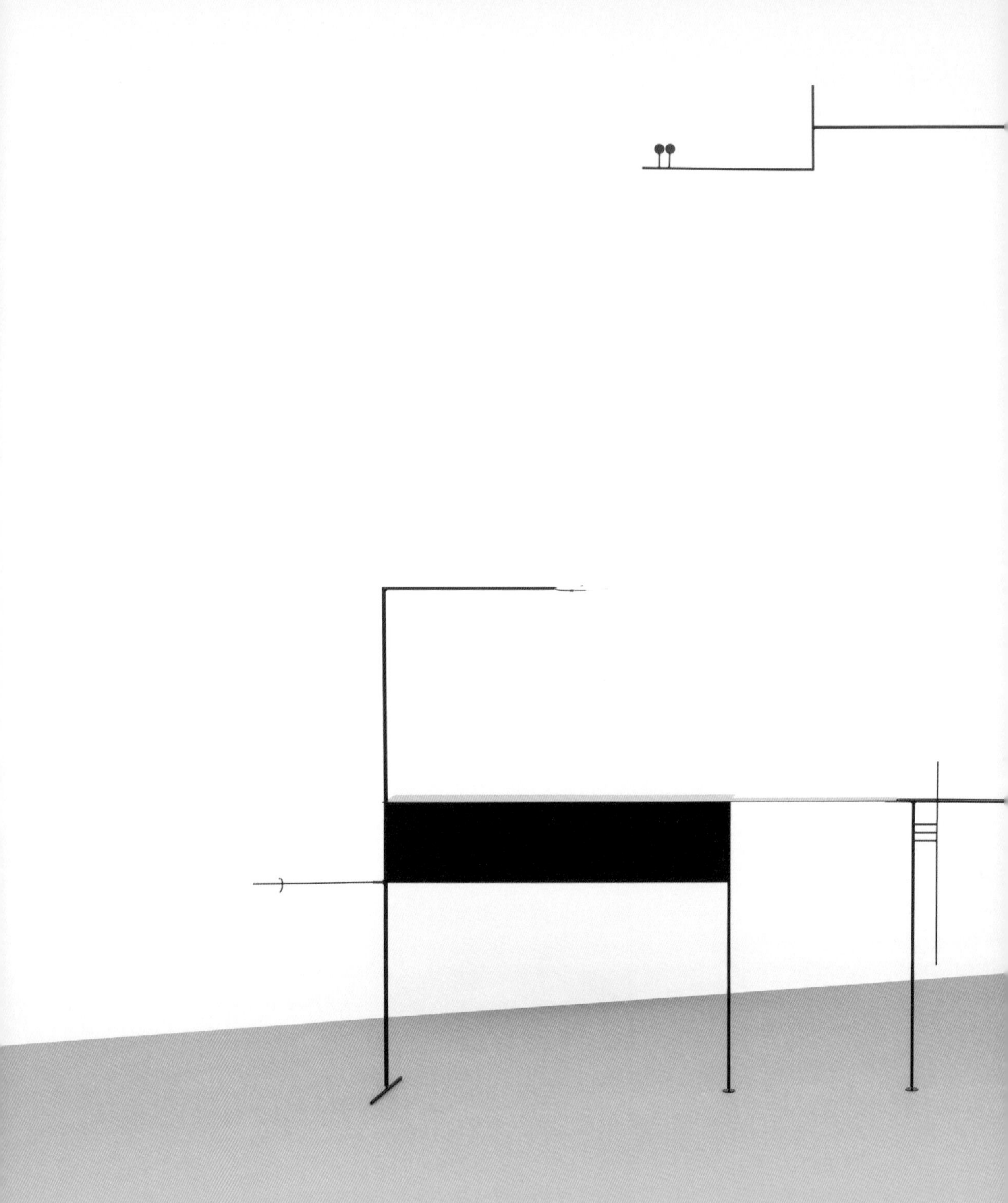

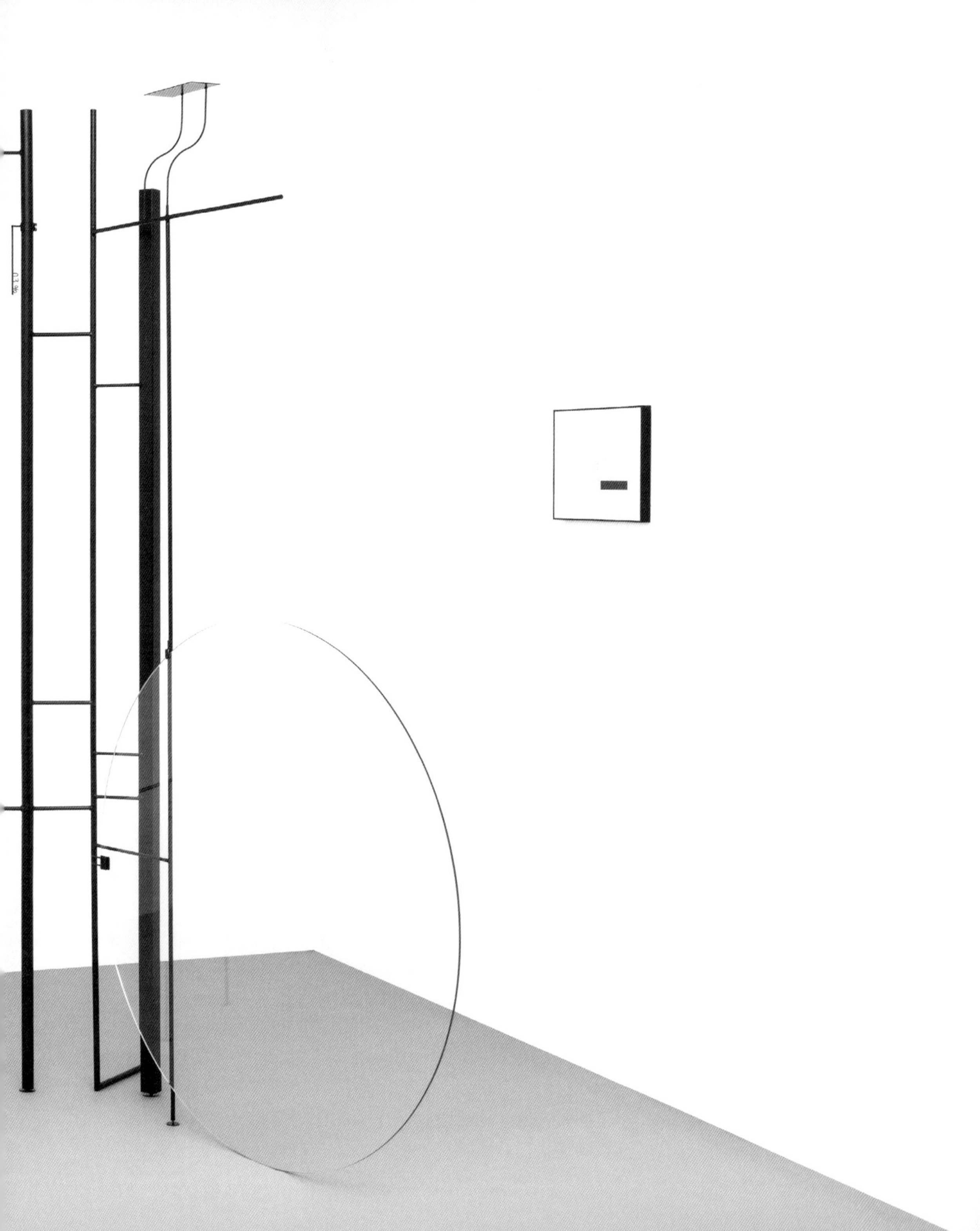

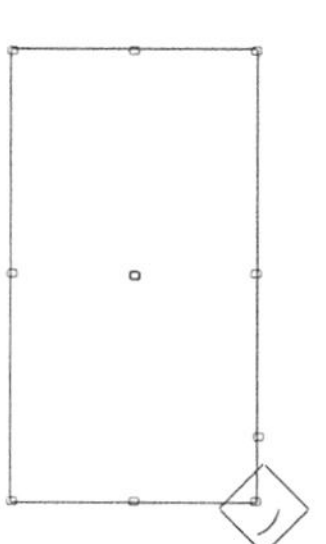

segment of shape inaccuracy
each appliance

unprotected 0
fig. 120 °

ingredients :

0,1%	measurement uncertainty
0,1 %	calibration
0,5 %	random error
0,1°	blunt angle
0,3 %	doubt

standart of shape accurancy
each value consists at least four independent measures

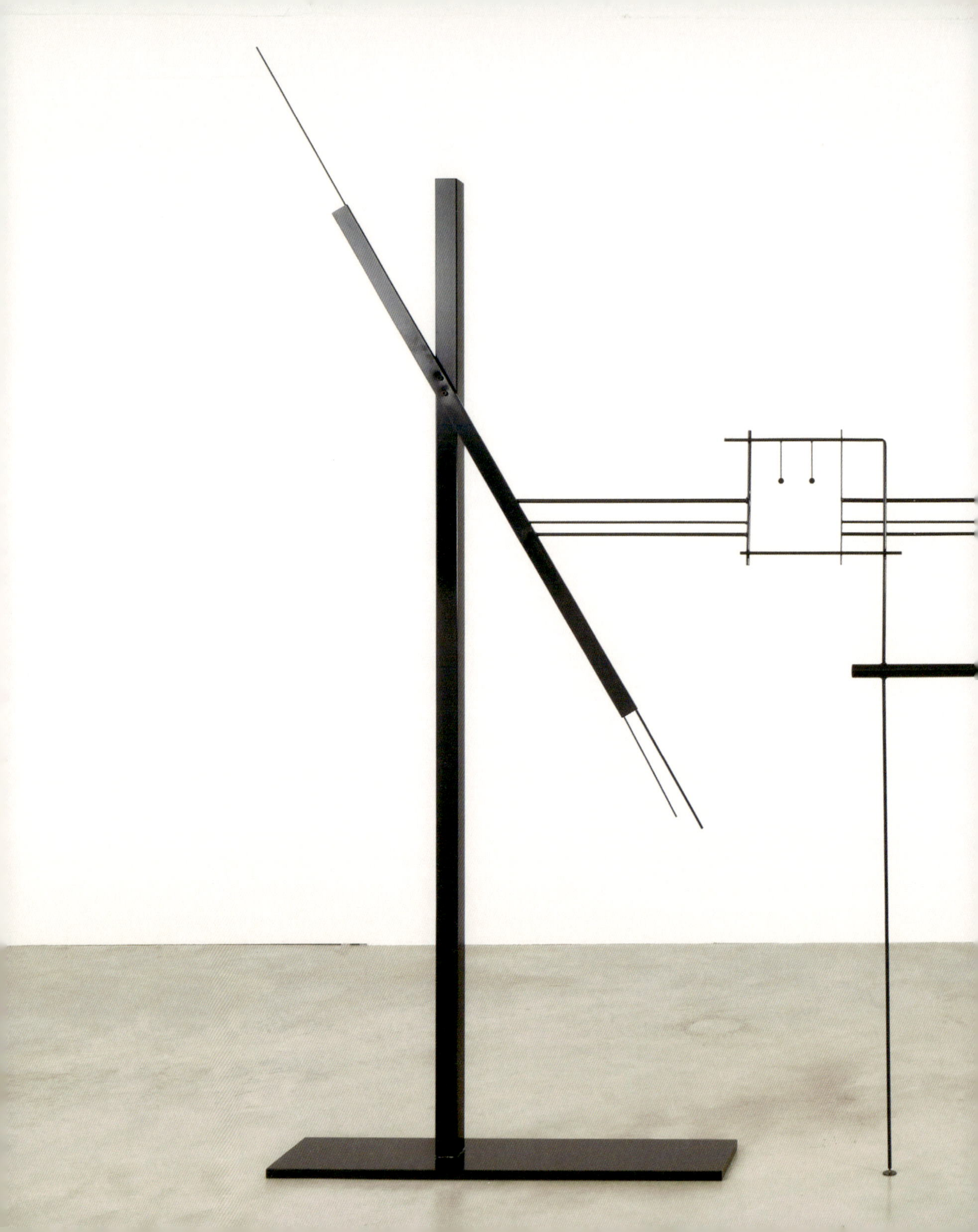

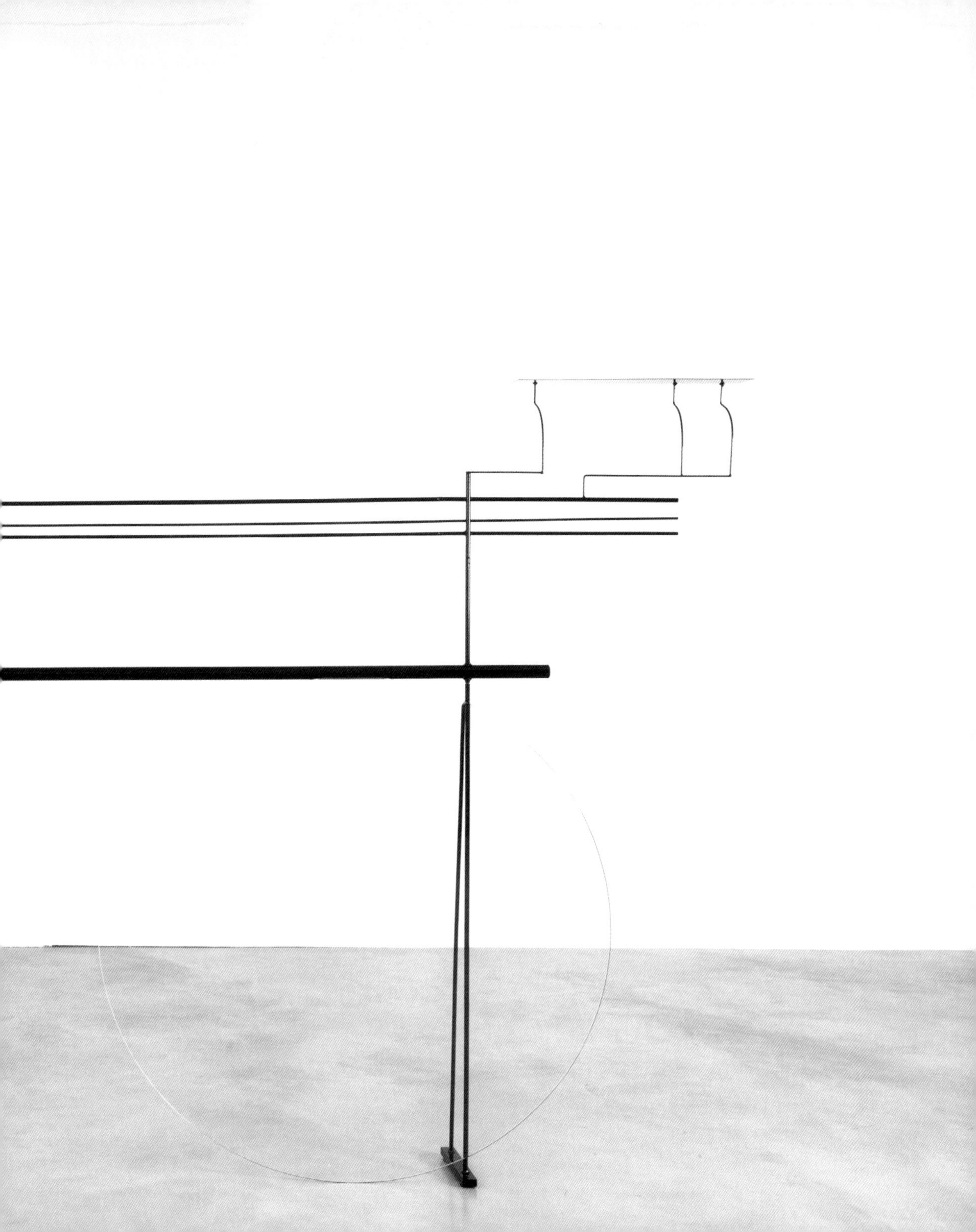

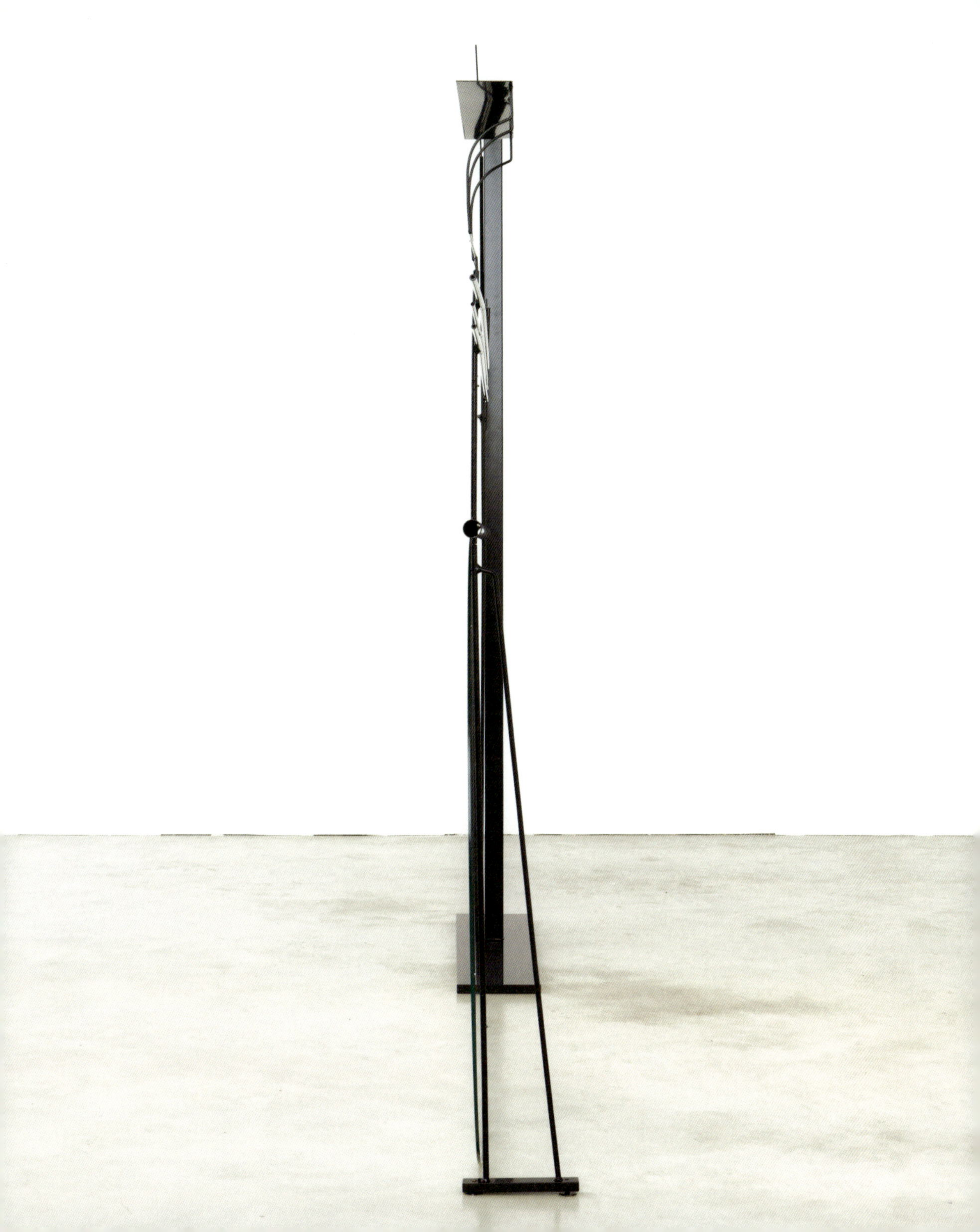

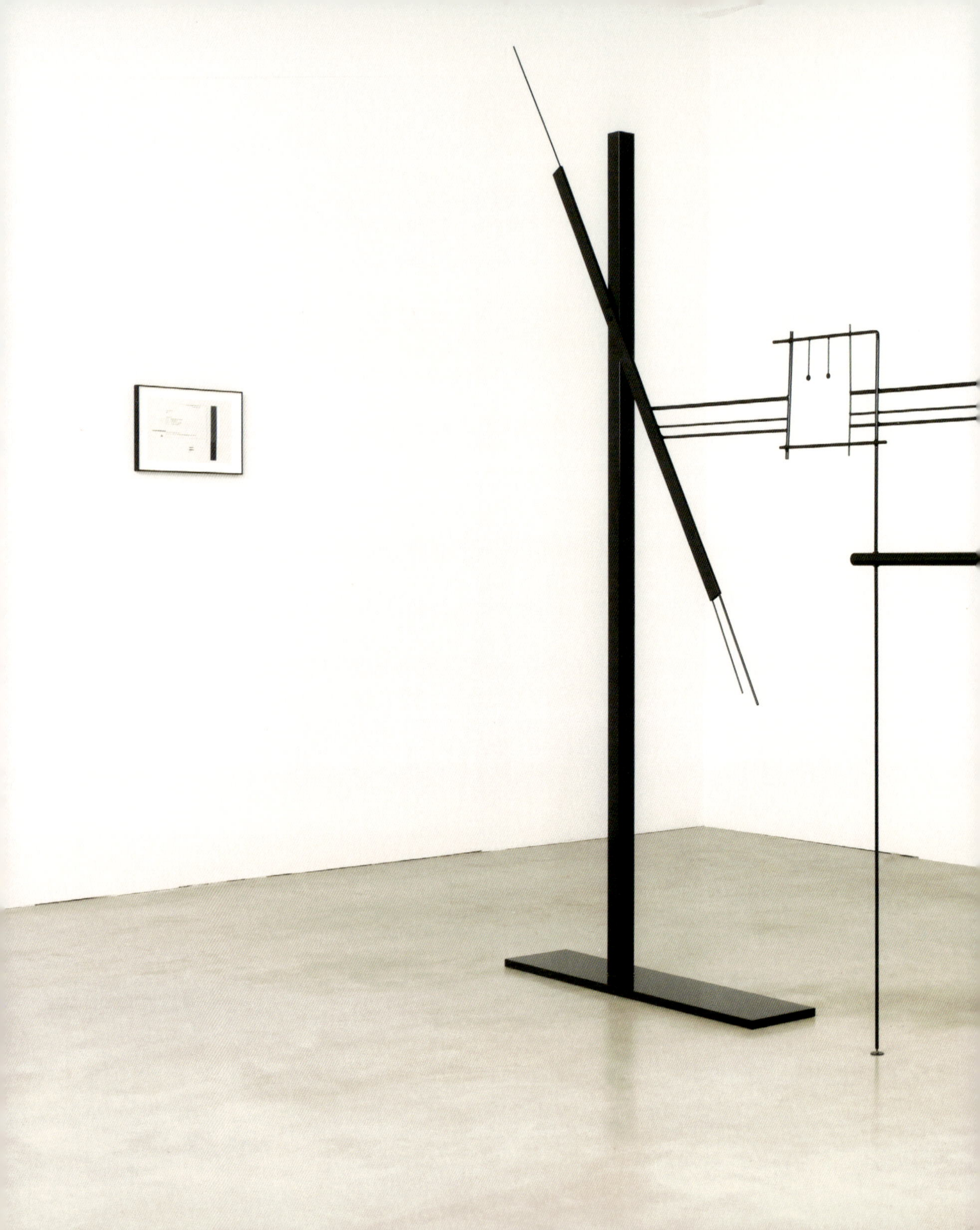

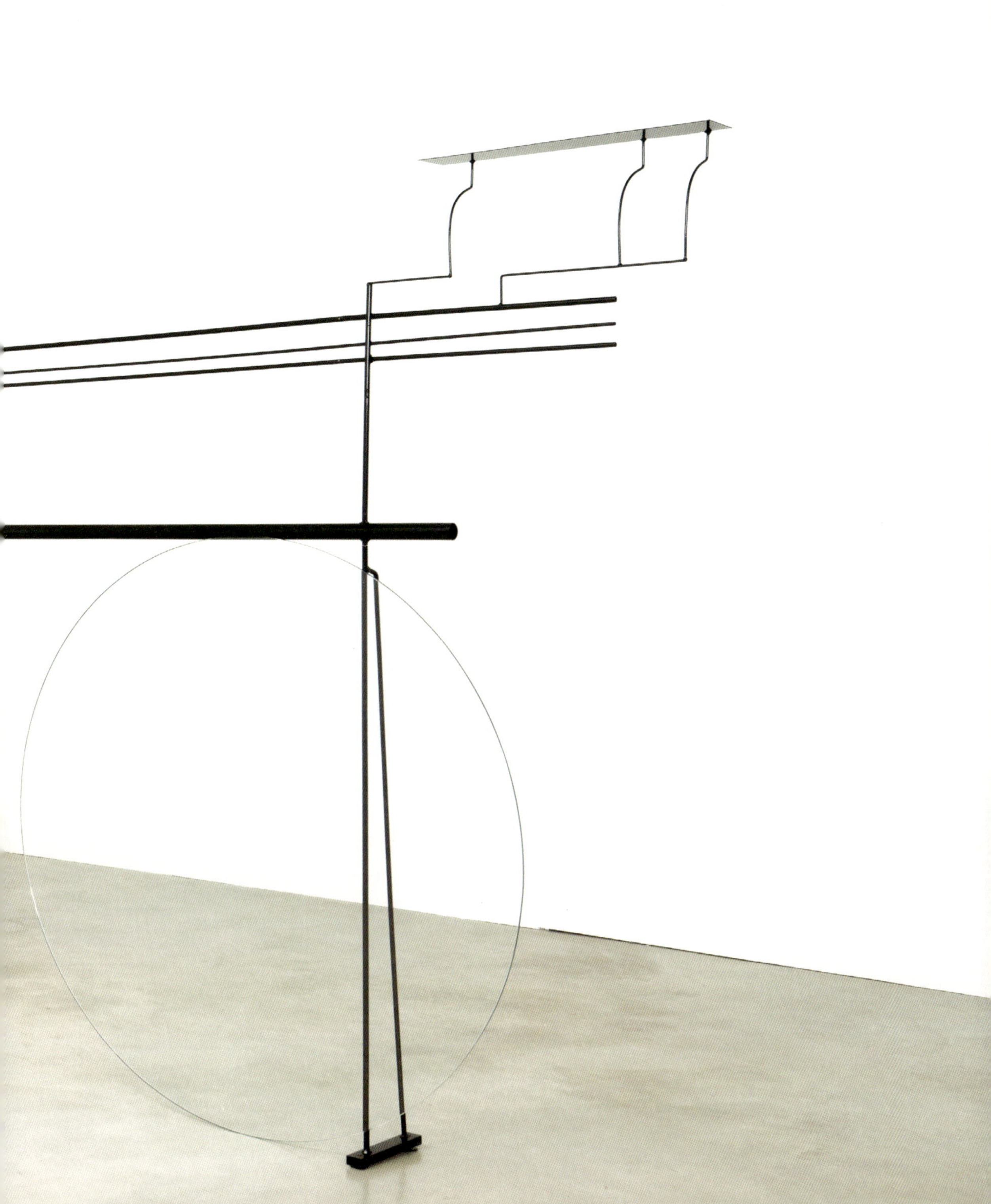

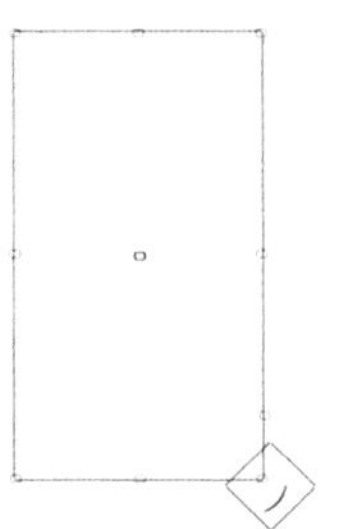

segment of shape inaccuracy
each appliance

unprotected 0
fig. 180 °

ingredients :

0,2%	measurement uncertainty
0,1 %	calibration
0,3 %	random error
0,1°	reference angle
0,5 %	doubt

standart of shape accurancy
each value consists at least four independent measures

shape hypothesis test	shape hypothesis test	shape hypothesis test	shape hypothesis test
A	0B	5.1	fx
2015, sculpture powdercoated steel 54 x 36 x 2 cm	2015, sculptural collage powdercoated steel glass 25 x 57 x 4 cm	2015, sculptural collage powdercoated steel 75 x 41 x 4 cm	2015, sculptural collage powdercoated steel glass 37 x 83 x 4 cm

shape hypothesis test	shape hypothesis test
f	1x
2016, sculptural collage powdercoated steel 28 x 63 x 3 cm	2016, sculptural collage powdercoated steel 48 x 41 x 3 cm

shape hypothesis test	shape hypothesis test	shape hypothesis test	shape hypothesis test
H	B	Y	9
2015, sculptural collage powdercoated steel 45 x 62 x 5,5 cm	2015, sculpture powdercoated steel 43 x 126 x 12 cm	2015, sculpture powdercoated steel 36 x 38,5 x 3 cm	2016, sculptural collage powdercoated steel 33,5 x 67,5 x 3 cm

S

"shape hypothesis test" series

I explore the intrinsic relationship between error and its derivatives, determining the degree of their presence in the sculpture to be made. For the series "unprotected 0", I created what I call "recipes". These recipes function as an index of what the sculpture is; much more than mere shape, it is the result of a causality that takes all contained ingredients into account. Knowledge and doubt, hesitation and precision, and the inaccuracies entailed, are all part of the process of creating a work: a percentage of errors, a percentage of uncertainties, a percentage of doubts, a percentage of angles, a percentage of shapes.

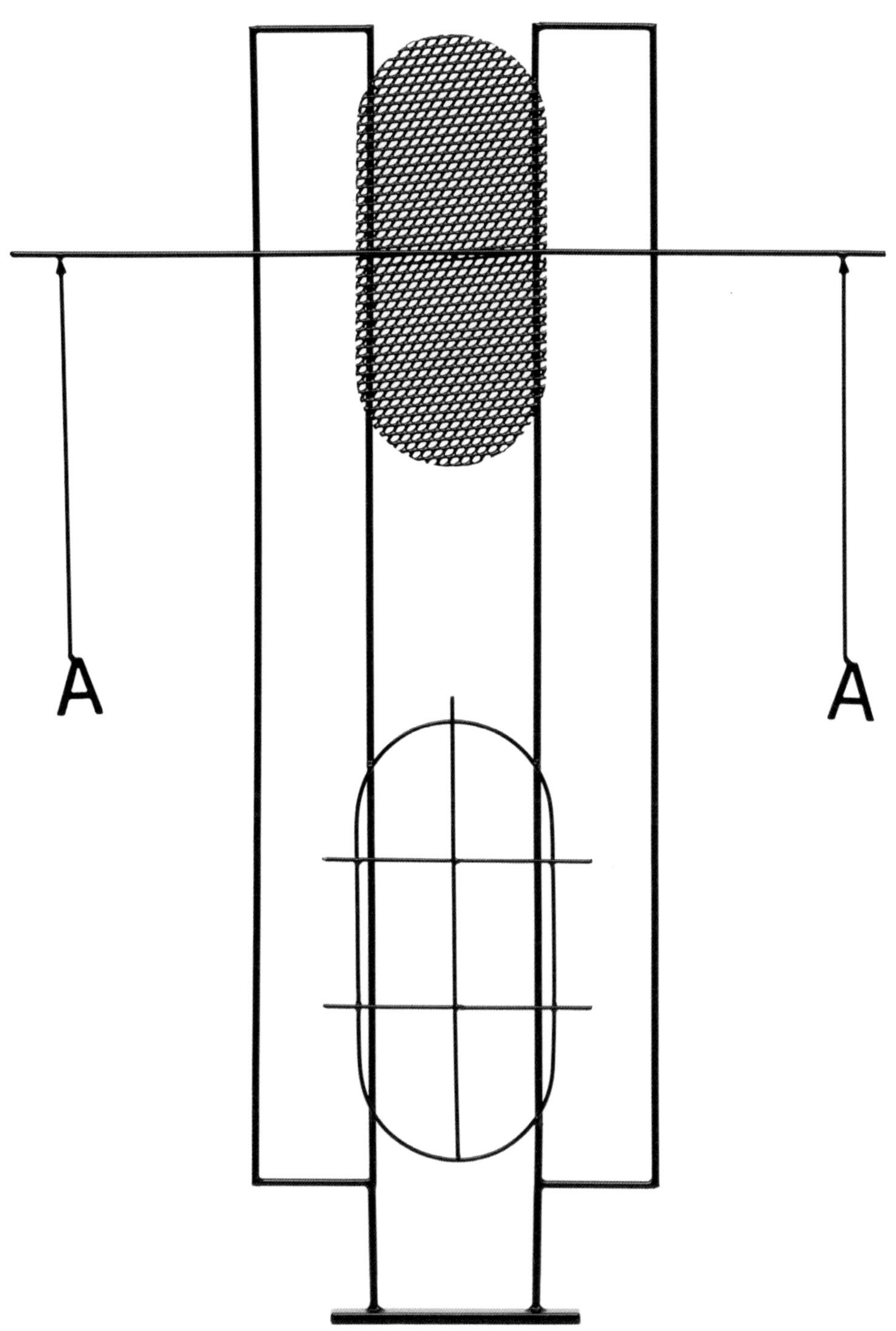
A
A

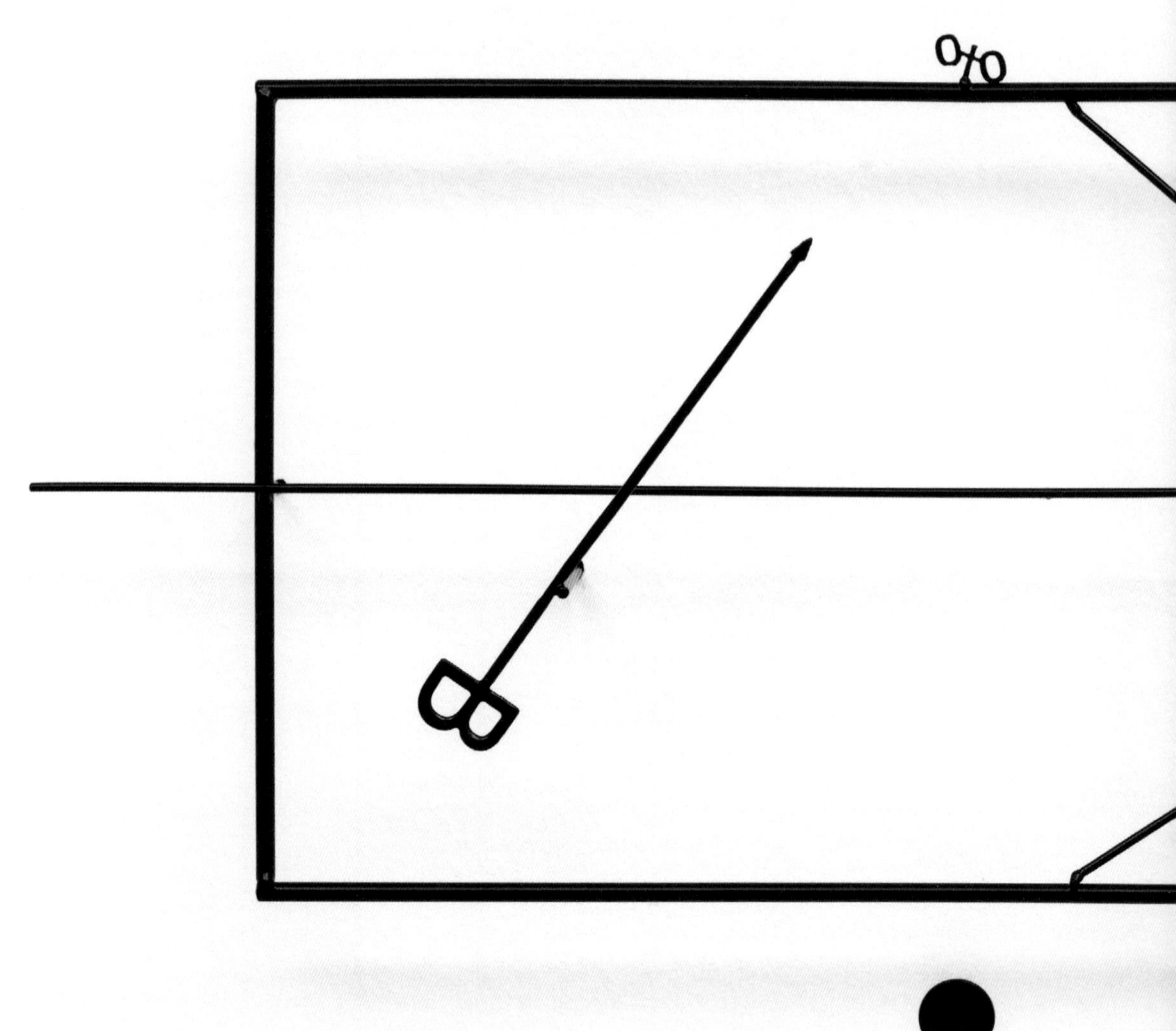
B

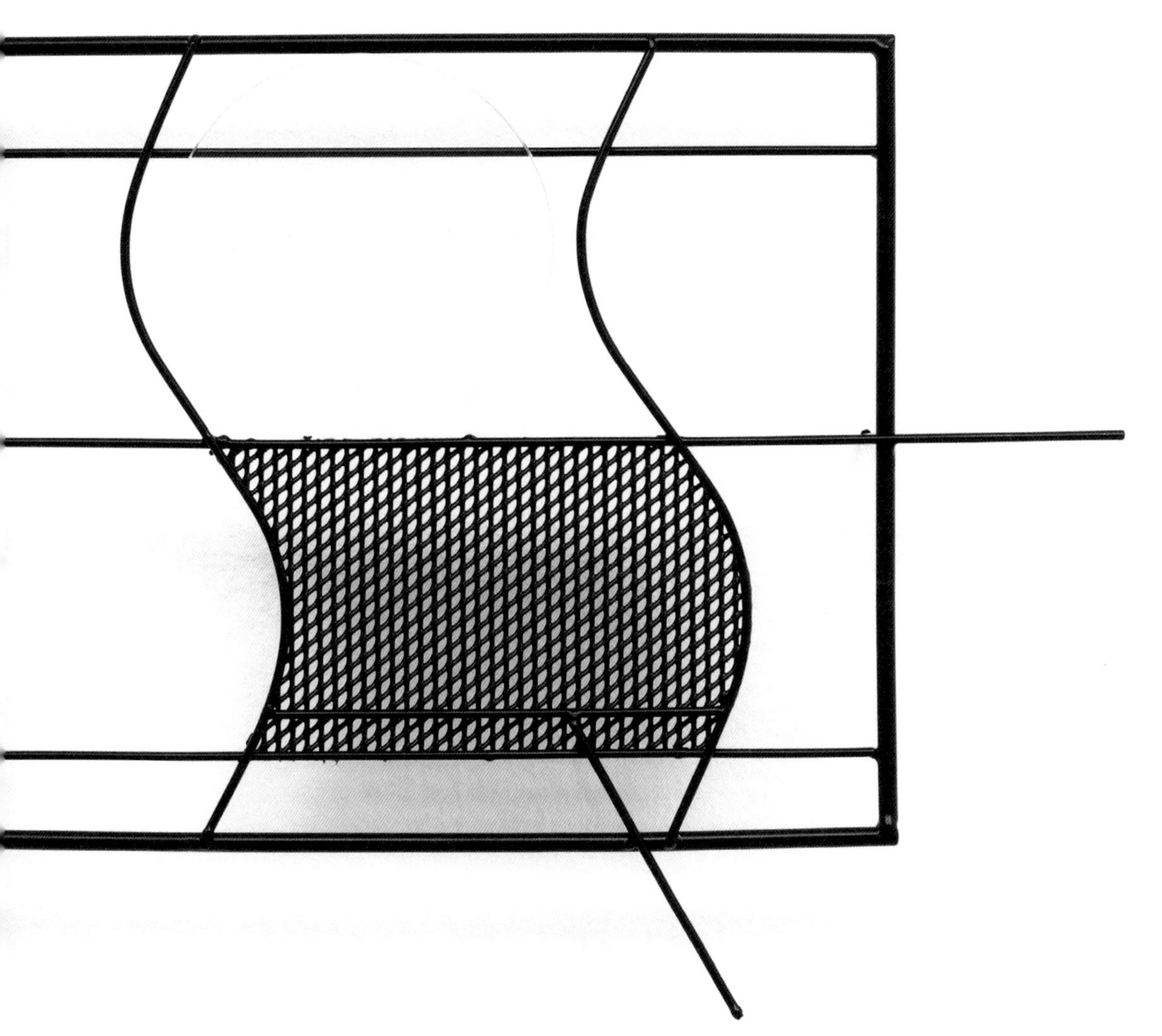

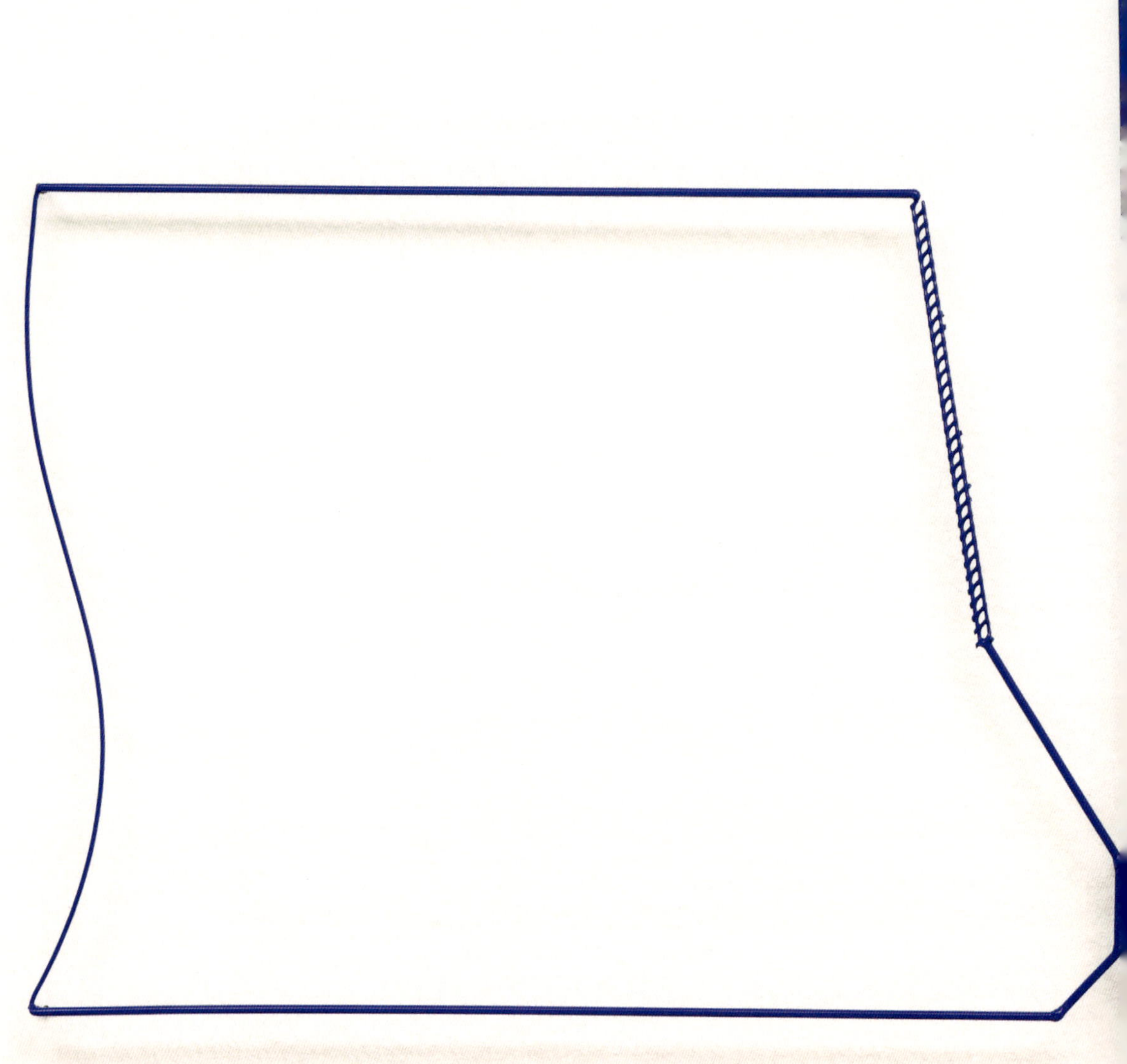

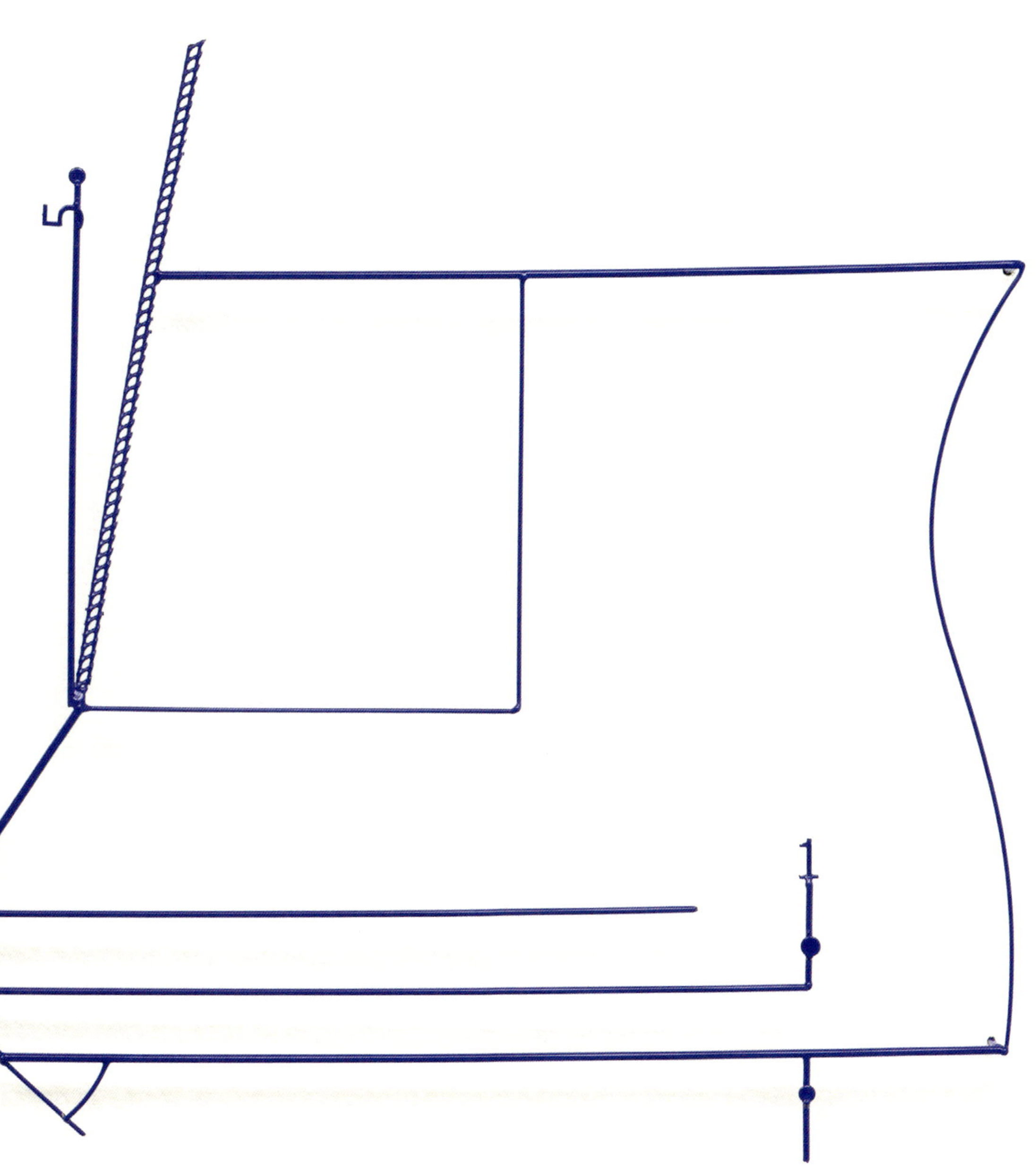

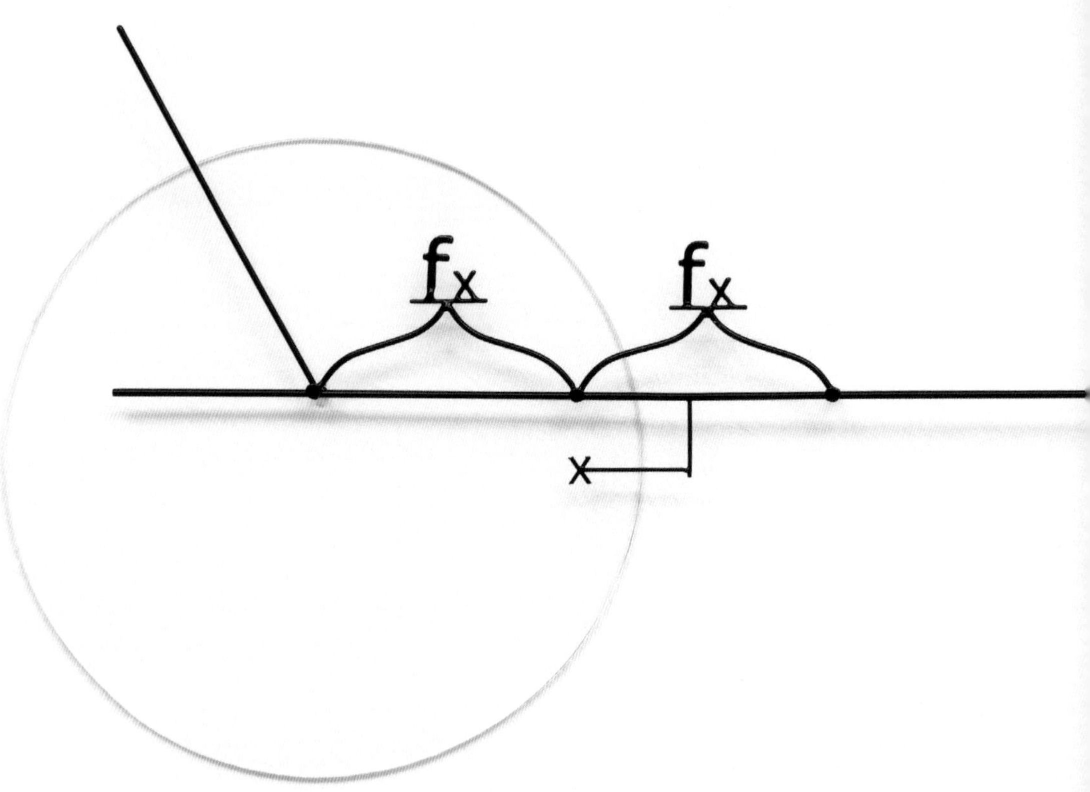
fx
fx
x

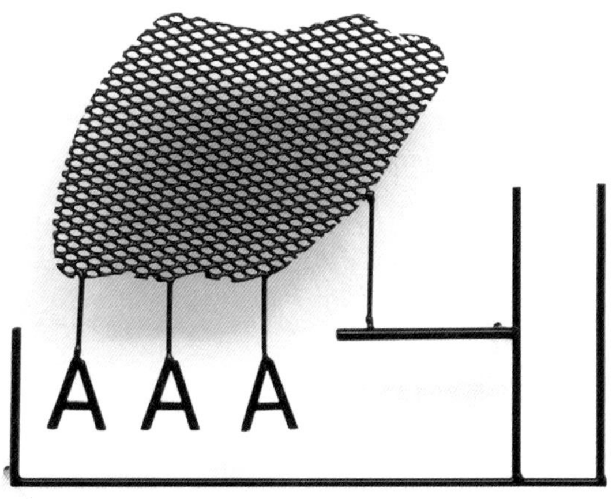
A A A

5

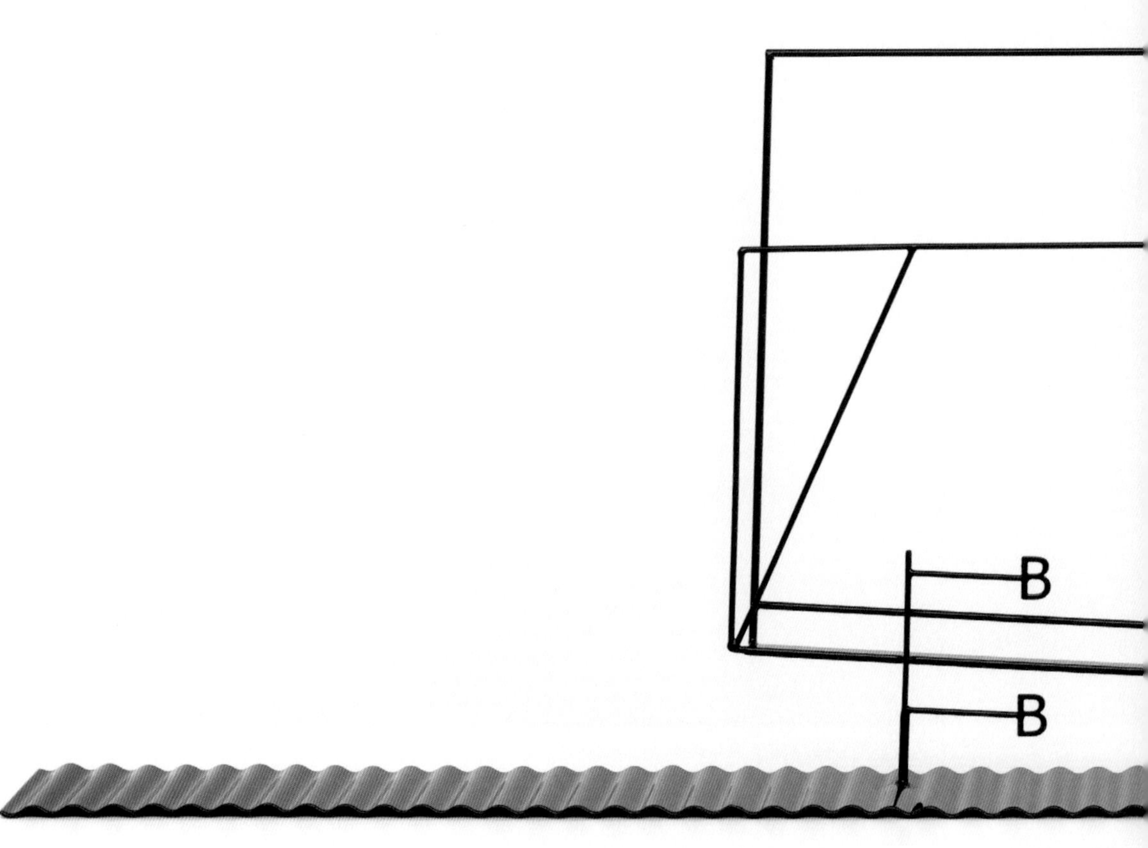
B
B

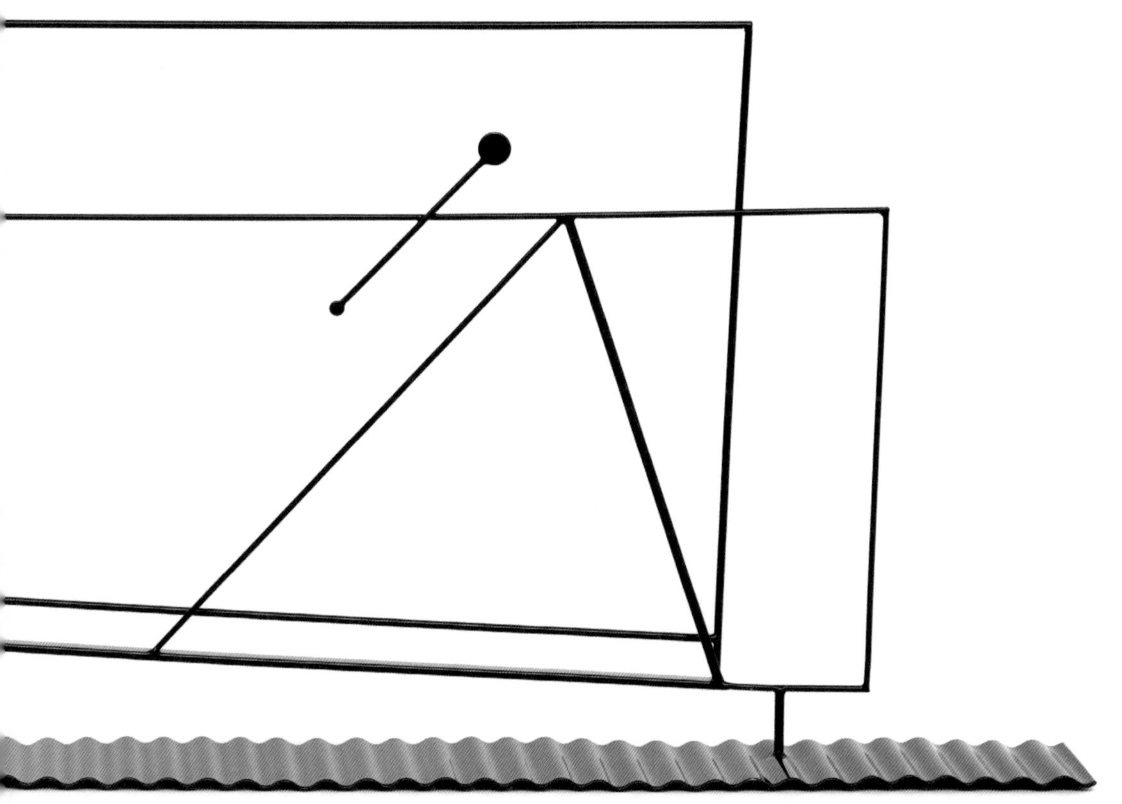

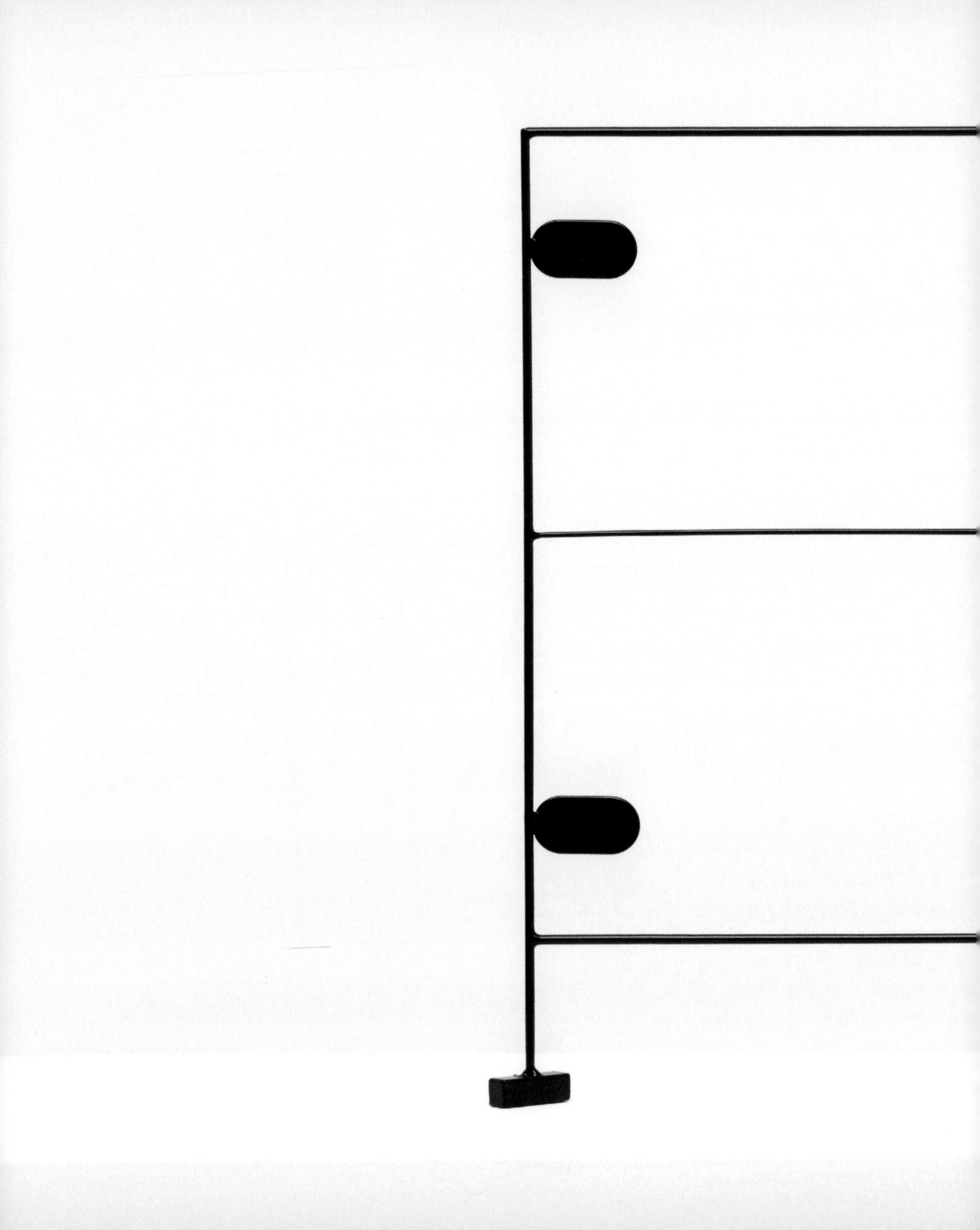

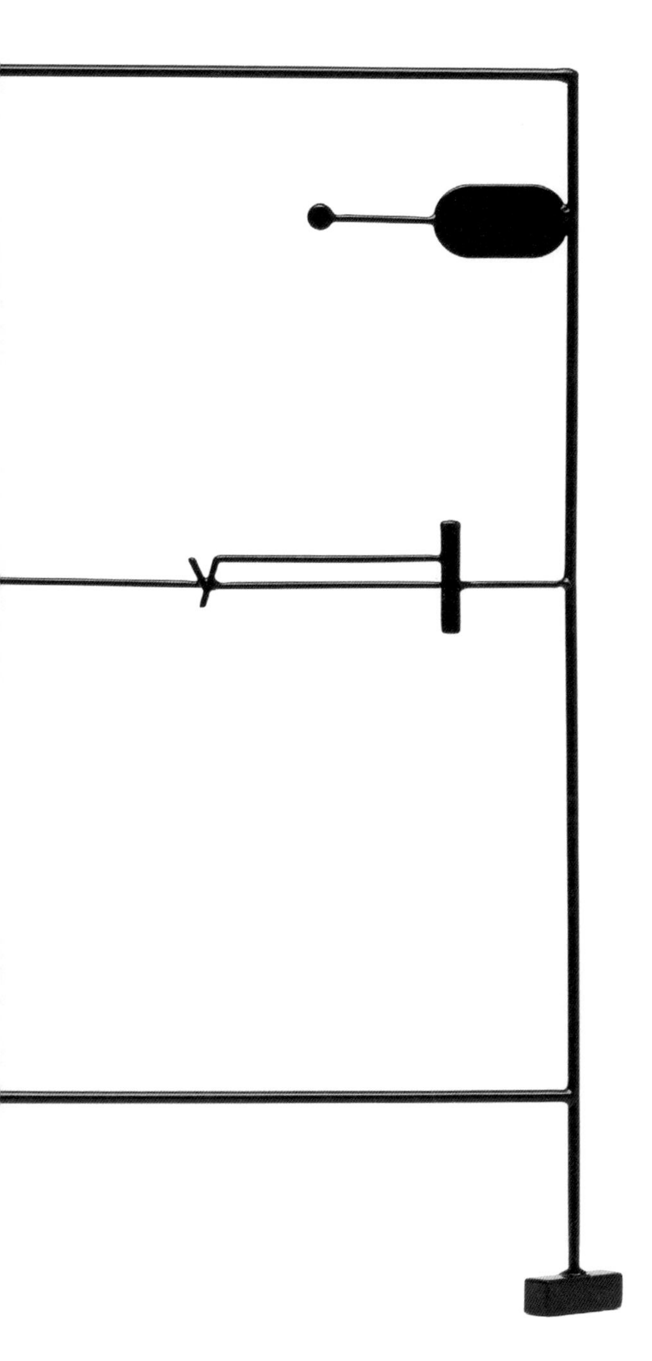

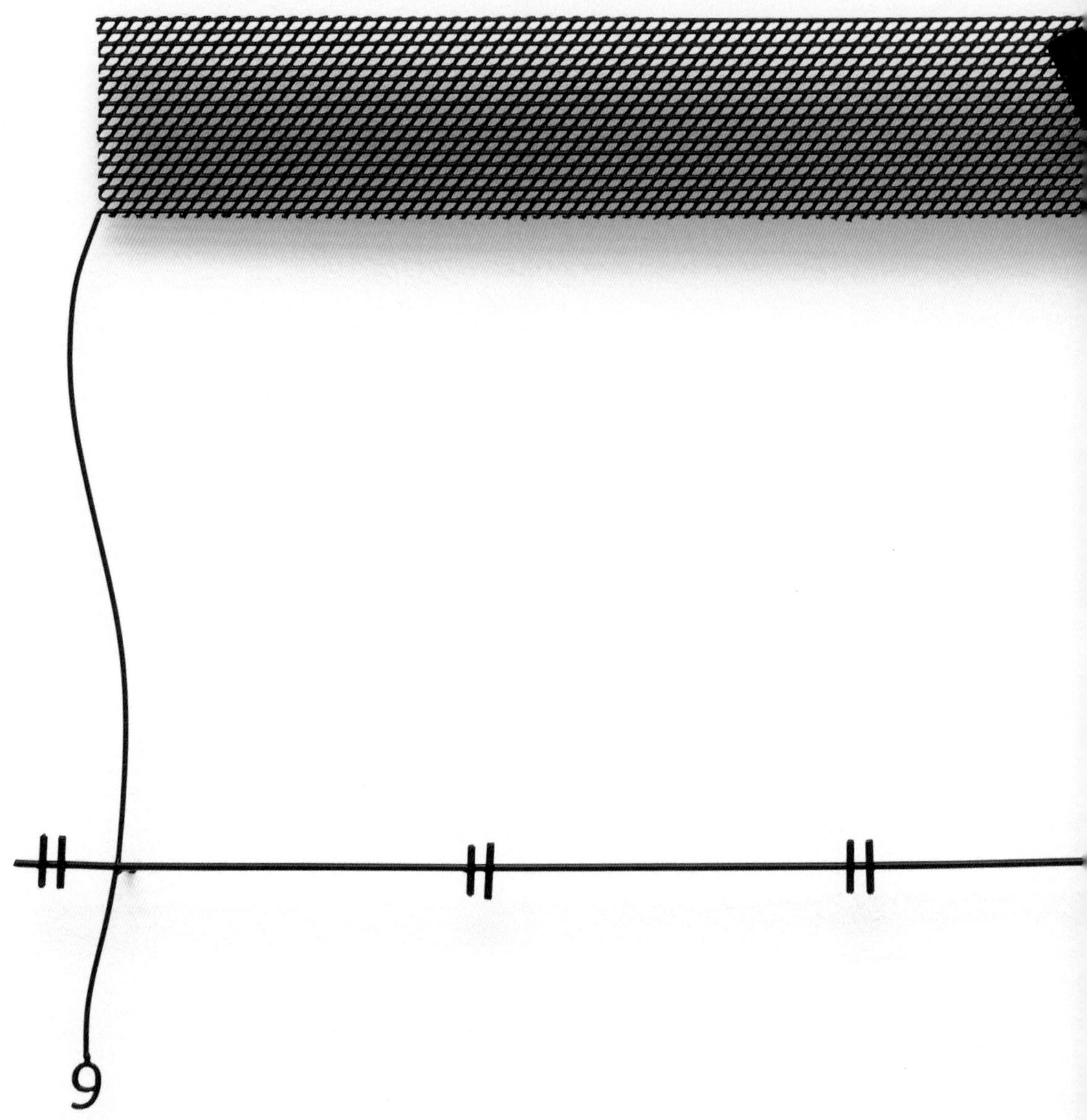

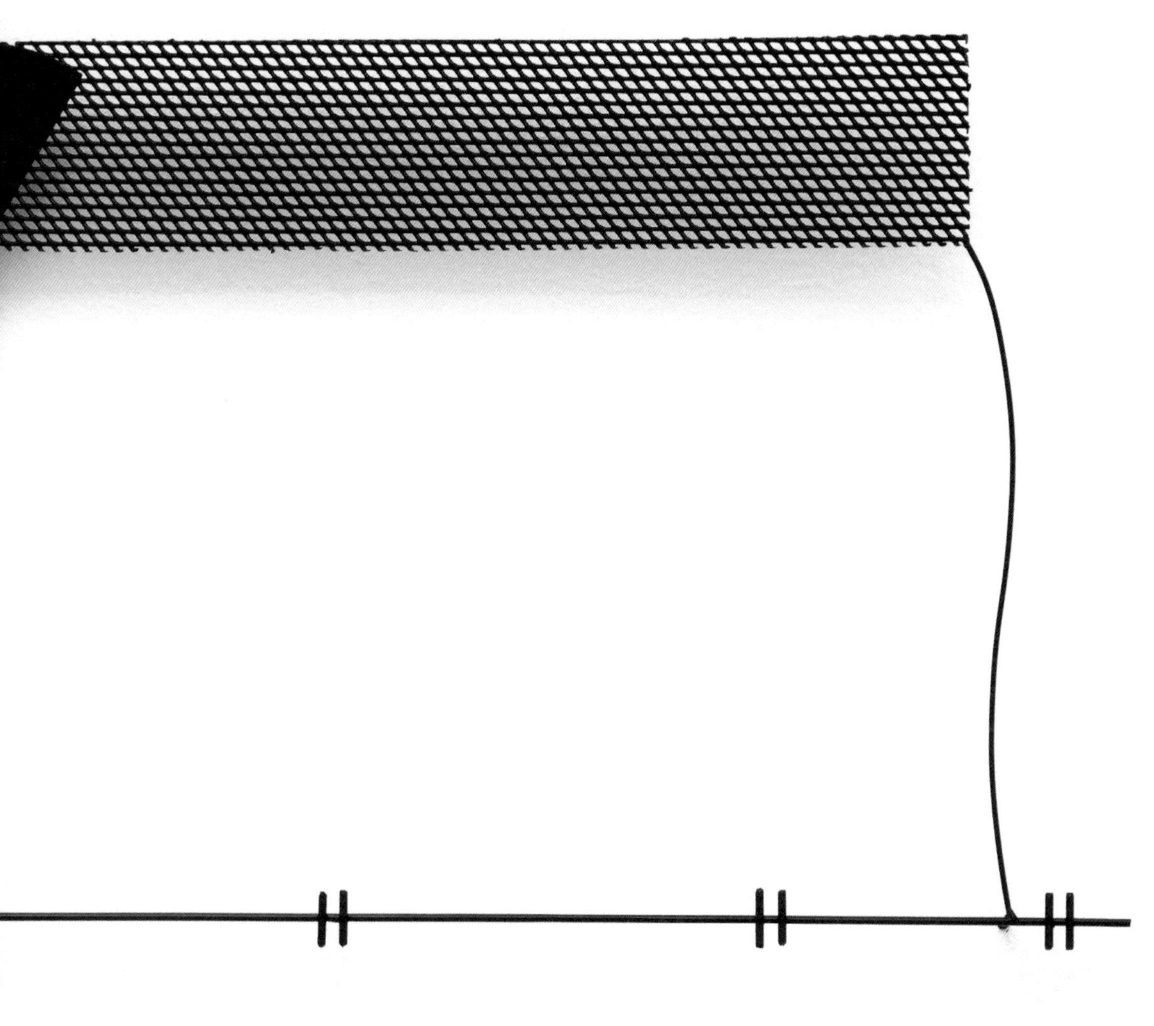

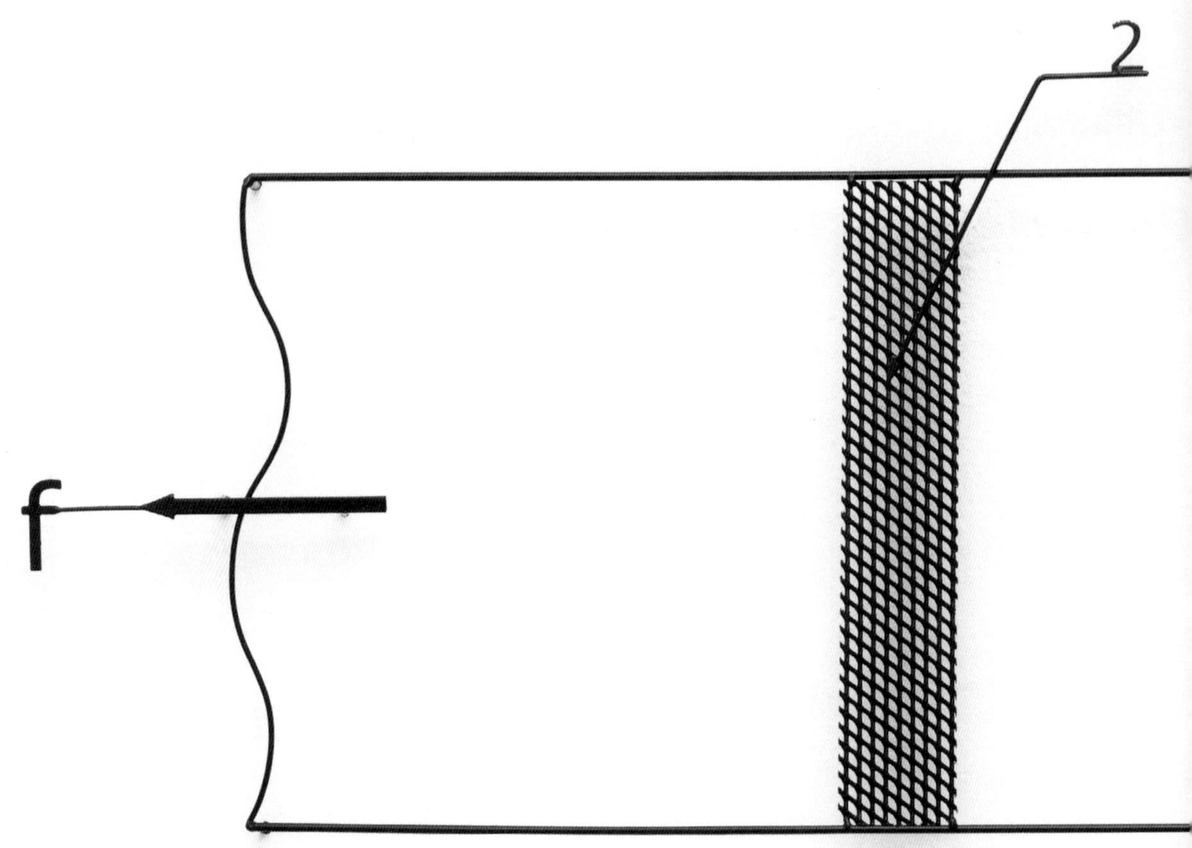
2
f

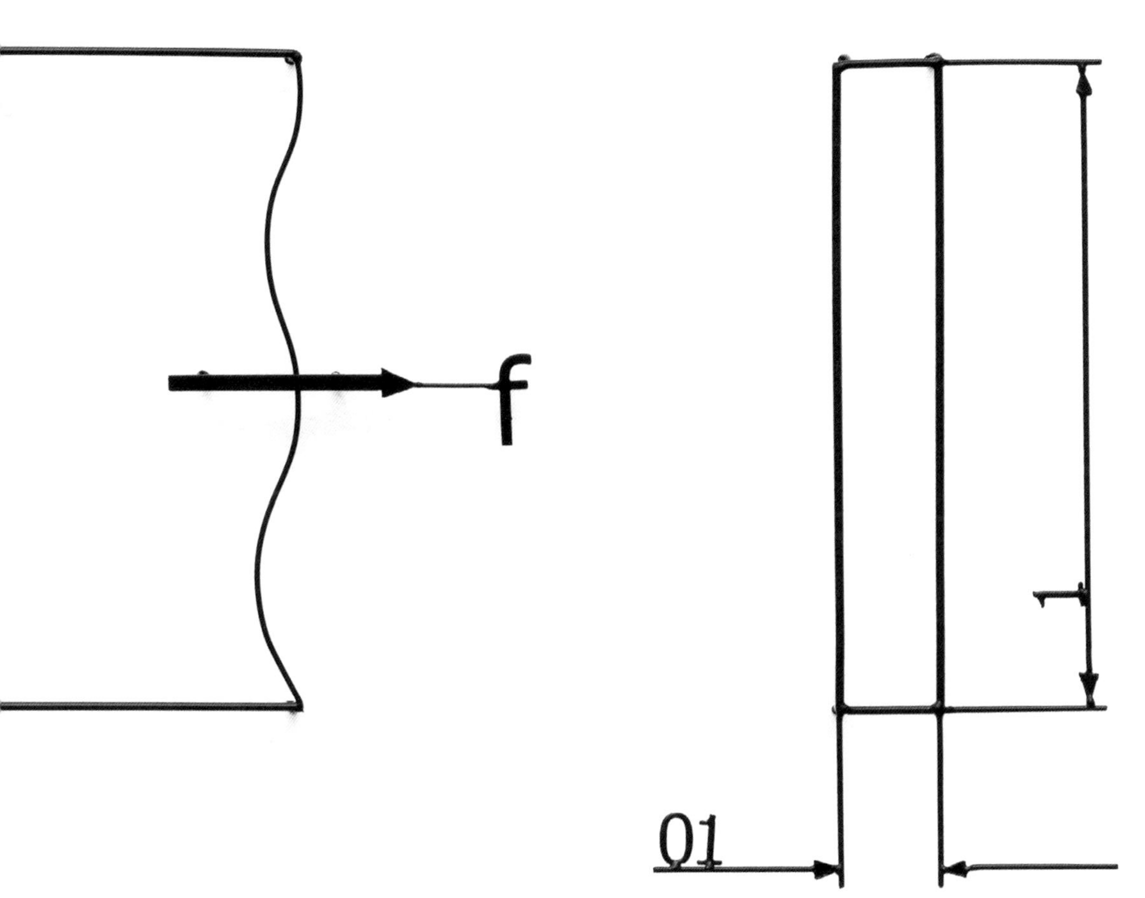
f

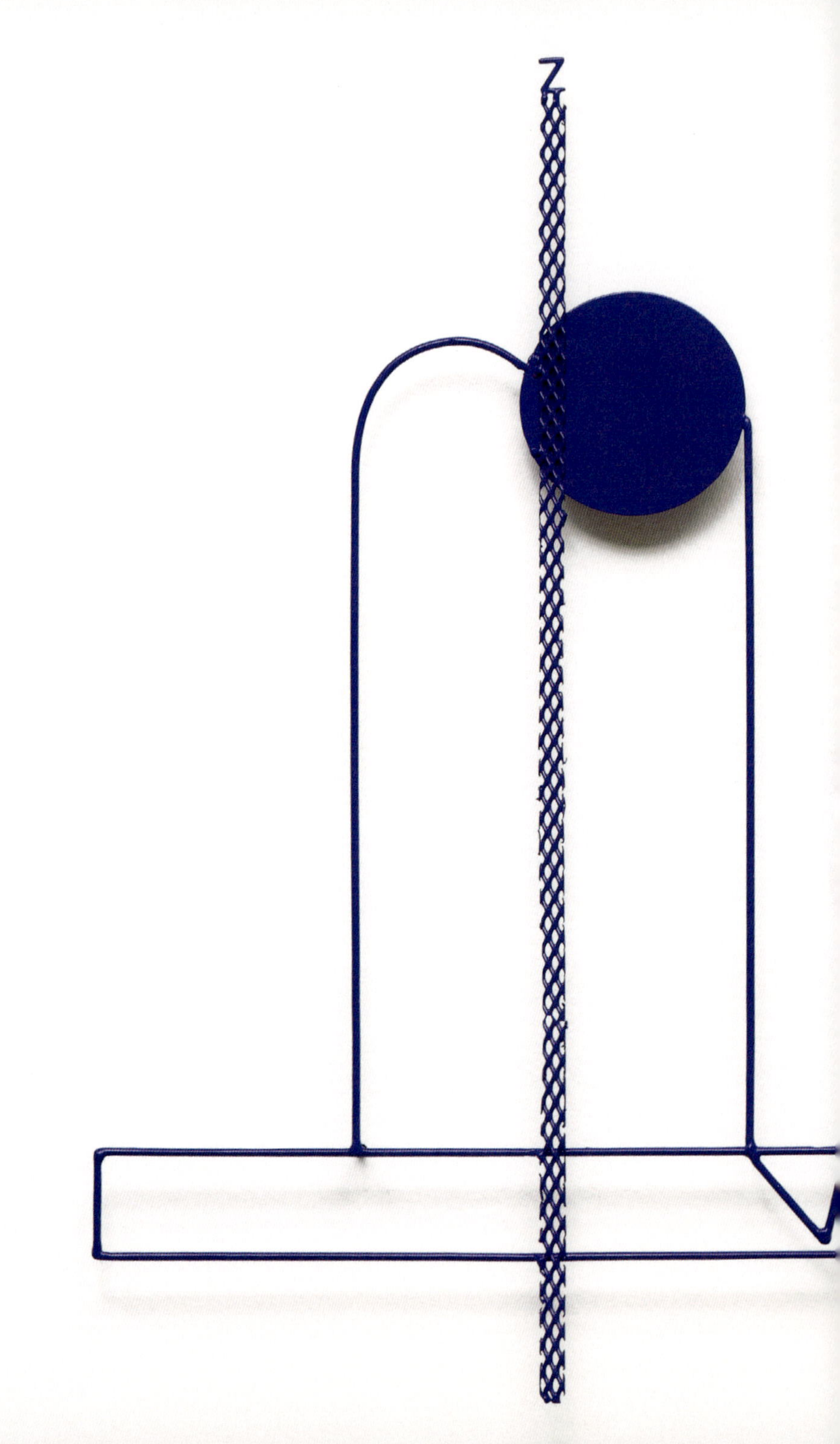

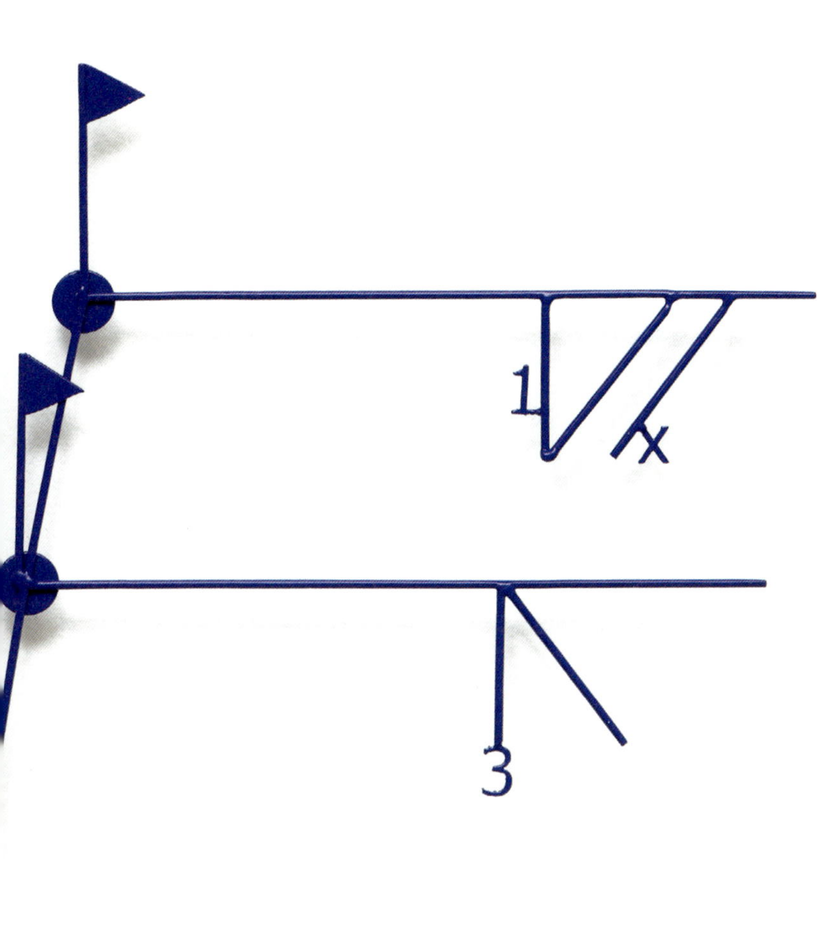

1
x
3

Lecture as a
contour of A.
The beginning
of shape

2015, sculpture
powdercoated steel
231 x 356 x 40 cm

In January 2015 I presented a lecture entitled “Lecture as a contour of A. The beginning of shape” at the TU Institut für Architektur in Berlin.

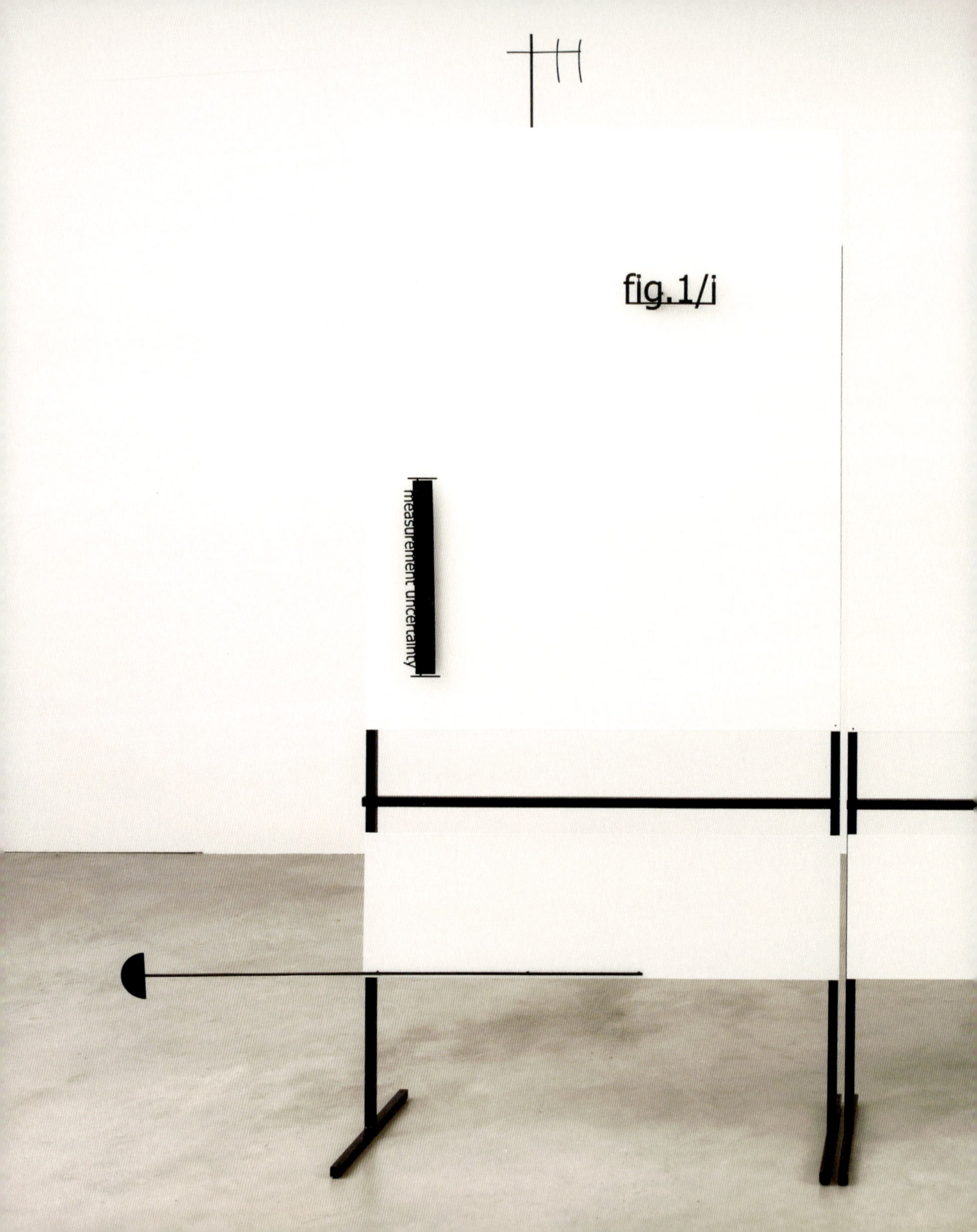
fig.1/i
measurement uncertainty

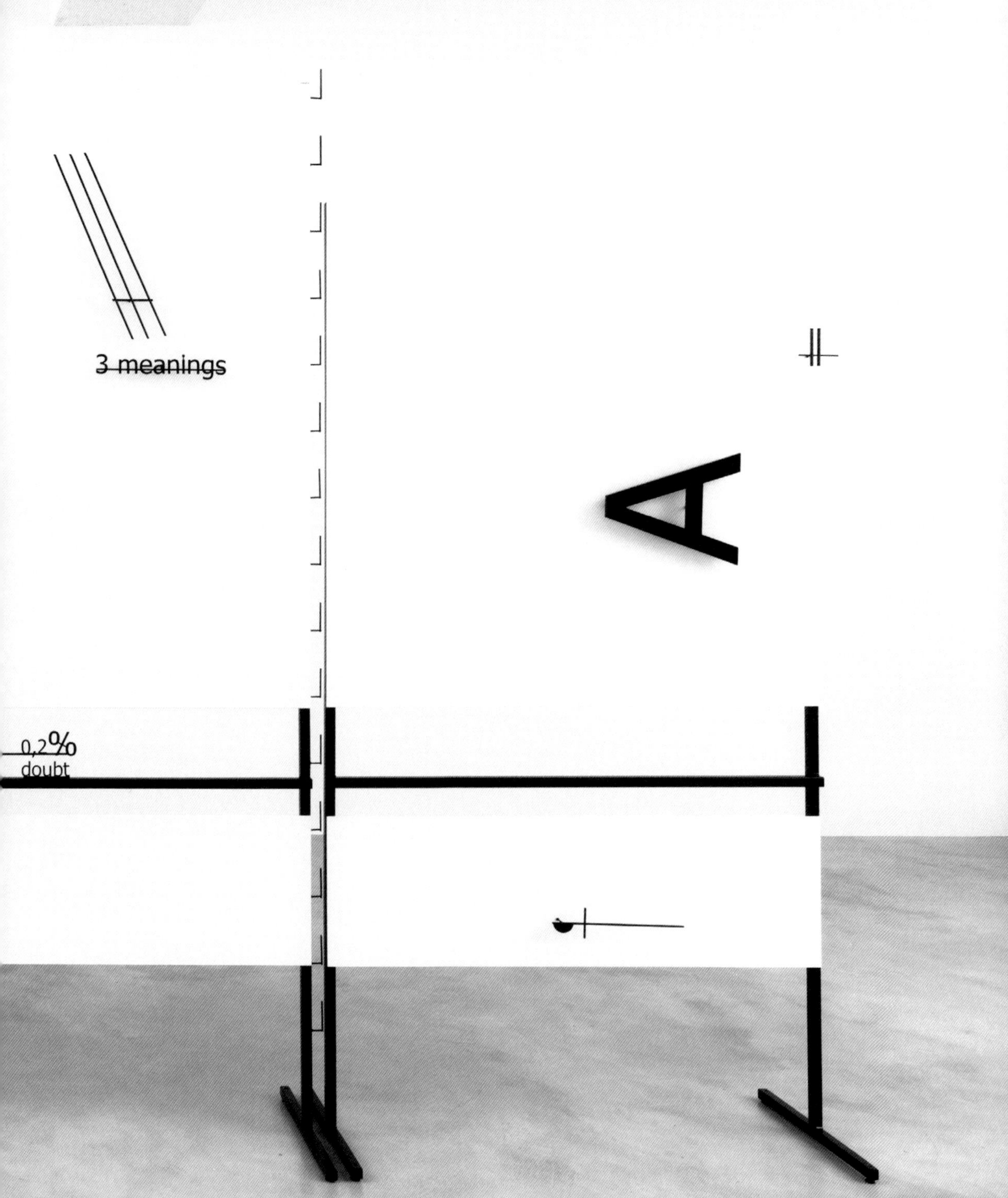
3 meanings
0,2%
doubt
A

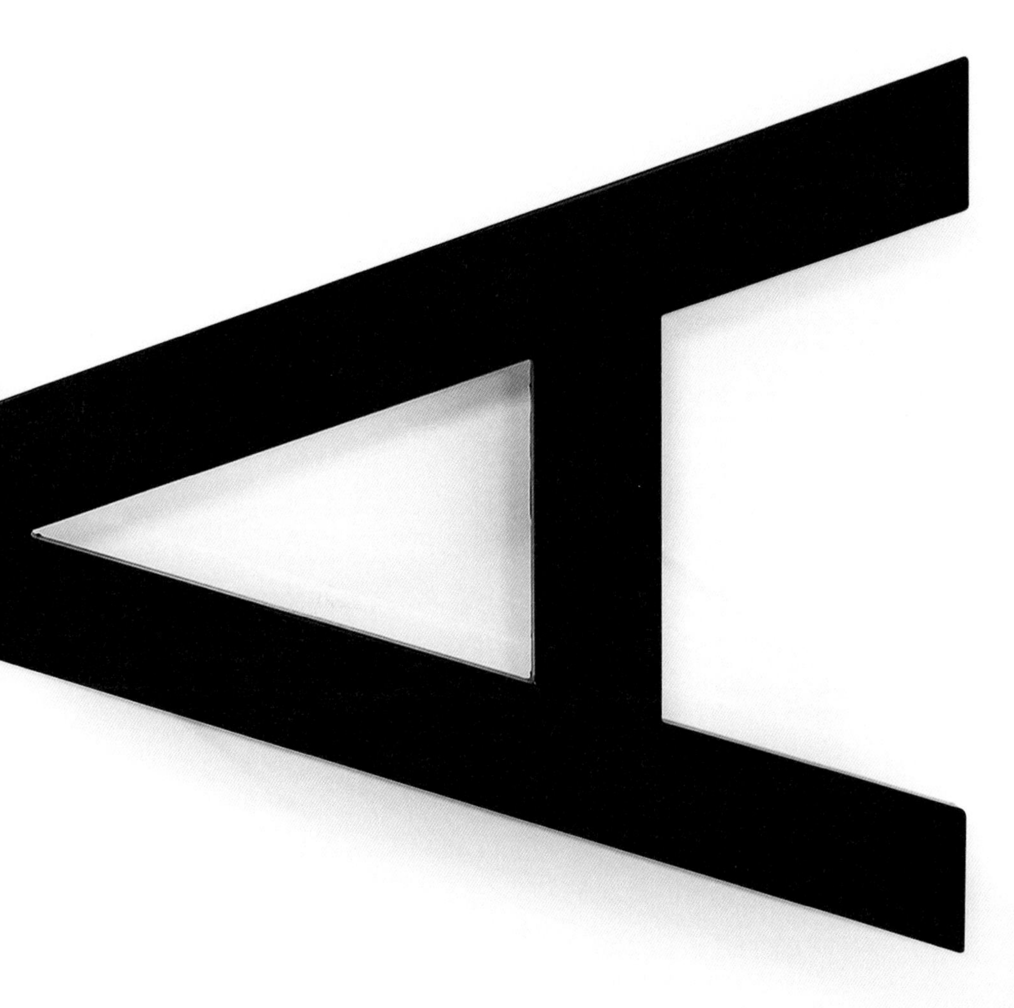

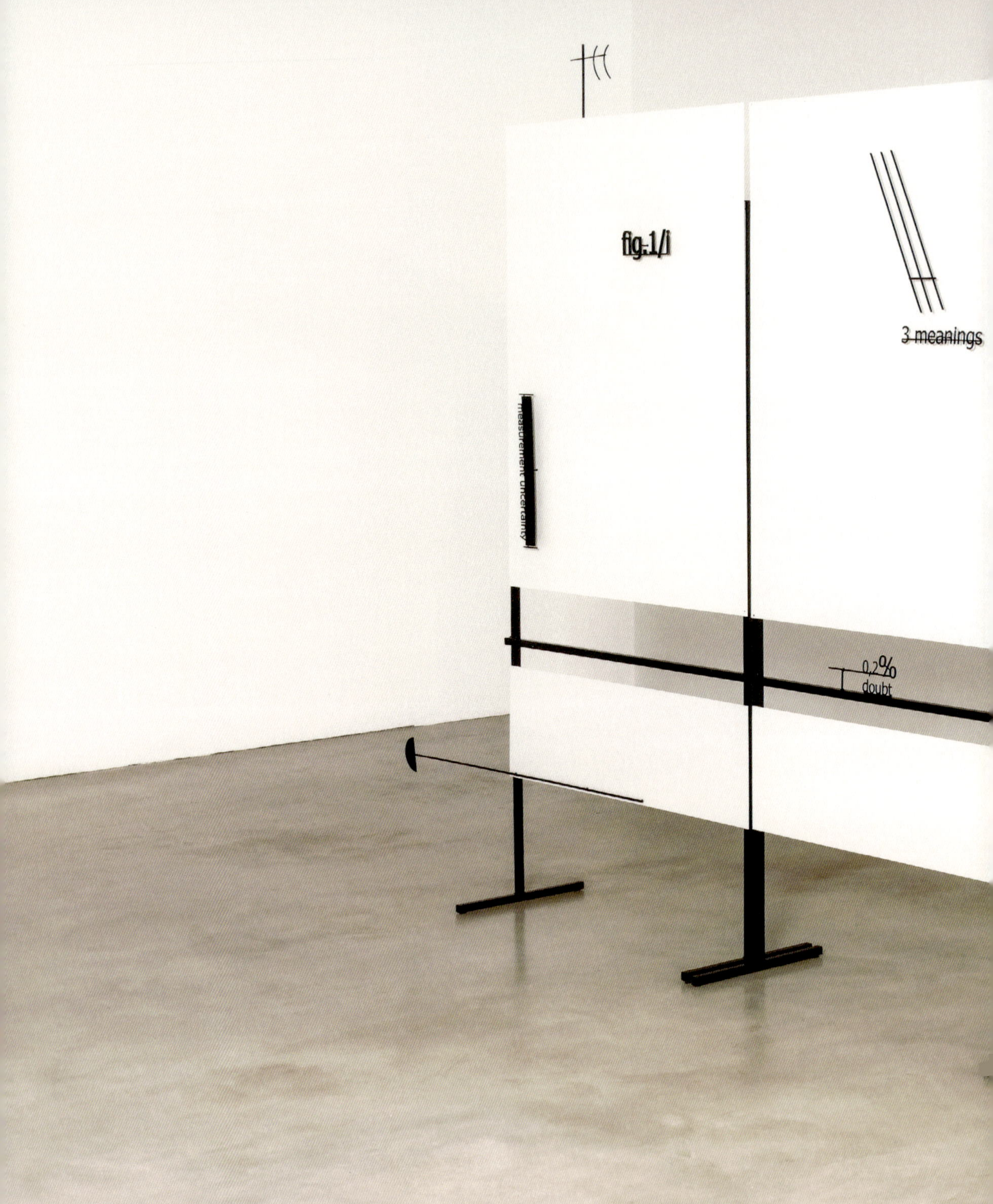
fig.1/i
3 meanings
measurement uncertainty
0,2%
doubt

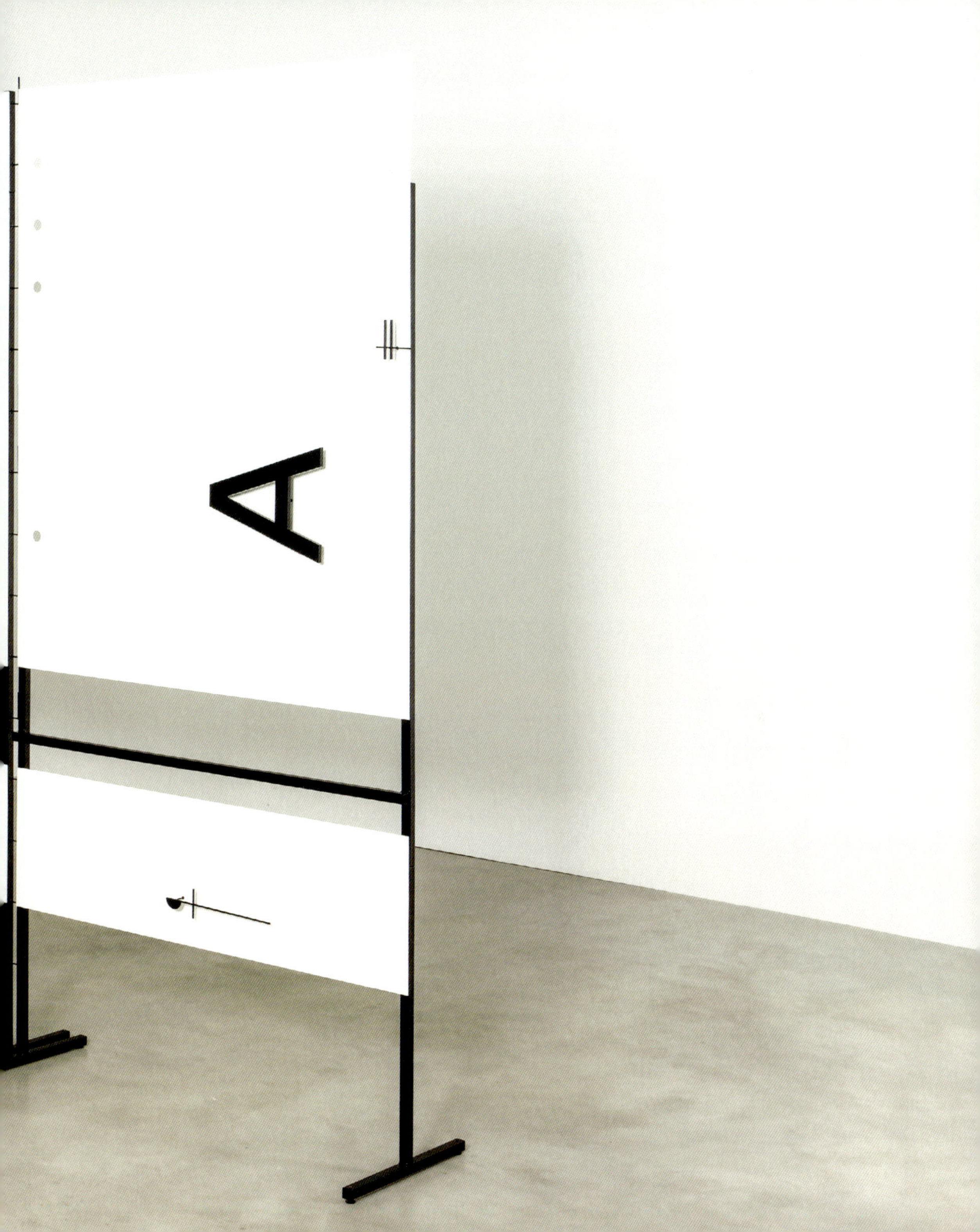

a divided dot	a divided dot	a divided dot
review	folder	N.01
2014 print 50 x 50 cm	2014, sculptural composition powdercoated steel print on paper 250 x 367 x 12 cm	2015, collage on paper steel, glass, print 42 x 29,7 x 3 cm

A

"a divided dot" series

A Typographic Point is the basic unit of measurement used for measuring font size and other typographical elements.

"a divided dot"

In the series of works entitled "a divided dot," I refer to the concept of Point in order to accurately define the geometry of space and its divisions into units and components.
In the "a divided dot" project, I carried out a detailed analysis of the Point, focusing on the situations in which the Point could be divided. The title itself, "a divided dot," already presents a spatial parameter, and functions as a form of sculptural language.
In this series, I construct forms using and arranging them into diagrams, algorithms, sculptures, and installations. The geometric and linguistic grammar of space is strictly defined by numbers, letters, and words that oscillate between precision and error. While the letters and words are used to describe space, the numbers are used to measure space.

Marlena Kudlicka
'a divided dot.review'

In her latest presentation 'a divided dot.review' Marlena Kudlicka reinterprets the concept of 'a review' as a further part of the 'a divided dot' project, which has been realized in her recent works.
The concept of 'review' represents another analysis of the chronology of the division point, which is also a review of the current exhibition and an overview of the previous exhibitions. Each edition expands the project into increasingly complex sculptural and language structures.
In the 'a divided dot' series, Kudlicka constructs her architectural forms using punctuation, letters, numbers, and words by arranging them into diagrams, algorithms, sculptures, and installations. Geometric and linguistic grammar of the space is strictly defined by numbers, letters and words that oscillate between precision and error. The letters and words are used to describe the space, while the numbers are used to measure it. An equally important function is played by the titles of the works, which Kudlicka treats as language sculptures.

The notions that were essential to maintain the continuity of the project were the chronology of the exhibitions and the issues that were presented in them:

Dot	•
Word	on.e
Sentence	'a divided dot'
Folder	'a divided dot.folder'
Review	'a divided dot.review'

from the smallest font, a dot to the text, review

A dot, the font, as the elementary printing unit, appears throughout the 'a divided dot' series. The 'Protocol of errors on.e' is a project which opens Kudlicka's sequence of works.
A dot in the word on.e functions as a mistake; at the same time this word has become the foundation for creating the free-standing iron constructions and a group of sculptural collages. The analysis of the dot is continued in the next 'a divided dot' presentation, which is an arrangement of the exhibition entitled 'Changing the Field of View. Modern Printing and Avant Garde" created for the Museum of Art in Lodz, Poland. The architectural grammar of the space, based on the principle of the counterpoint, resulted from its close connection with the notion of the Typographic Point. The 'a divided dot' sentence, constructed of solid figures, which have been derived from the shape of letters, has been placed by the artist in the 400m2 museum hall in accordance with the strict rules of the Strzemiński and Tschichold functional printing. Placed in a rectangular contour of the museum walls, the sculptures have formed a three dimensional model of the catalogue cover.
In the 'a divided dot. folder' presentation, Marlena refers to the idea of the folder as a collection, in which she archives and documents the mechanisms of division of dot and its components.

The concept of a review is another segment in the construction of the 'a divided dot. review' project, which, as a new element in the arrangement of the exhibition, co-creates, summarizes and expands the concept of the exhibition.

The 'a divided dot.review' project is a site-specific work. For Kudlicka the exhibition room becomes a typographical field, which has been converted into a magazine of art, and the planes of the walls function as its part. The graphic and text form has been laid out on a moving wall playing the role of a card opening in the catalogue. The excision of the lower part of one of the walls in the gallery can be associated with the fold of a page which is just being read. The digits placed in the corners of the walls, used by the artist to sharpen the precision of the space, represent the page numbering in the magazine of art.
The composition of a review is tailored to the thematic requirements of the work, the intended recipient, the specificity of the medium in which the review has been published. Reviews belong to the group of metatextual genres. They are preceded by another sender's statement, which becomes the object of description and critical reflection. Both acts of communication are, by definition, separated by the distance in time. The outcome is a text that has two authors (the author - the creator of the message, the reviewer - critical reflection on the message). Art reviews are almost always written after the work has been made public (by exposure or print) (Wiki)

№

In the case of the 'a divided dot. review' exhibition, the above defined notion of distance loses its meaning: the artist presents the text of the reviewer. Another thing is the disappearance of the division into the review and the work: a review as a concept becomes a tool, which is transformed into a spatial linguistic composition.

In the context of the analysis of the 'a divided dot. review' work, the 'review' structure represents a type of a closed composition, characterized by a strong connection between the text components. An important role is also played by the title of the exhibition, which introduces its theme and reveals the main thesis.

A review plays analytical-critical and informative functions, but for Marlena it is not a standalone description of a work, but, analyzed as the concept itself, it becomes the medium, part of the exhibition, and in fact the exhibition itself. In the 'a divided dot.review' project the distinction between the form and content does not exist. Jacek Kowalski 2014

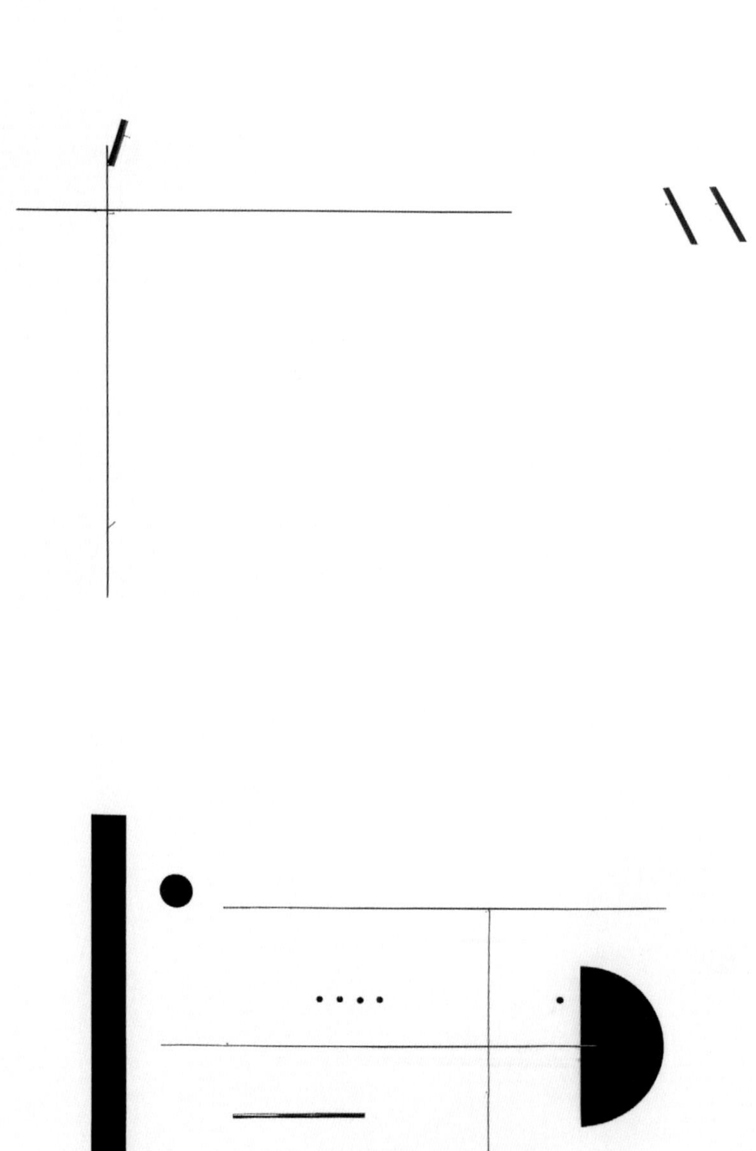

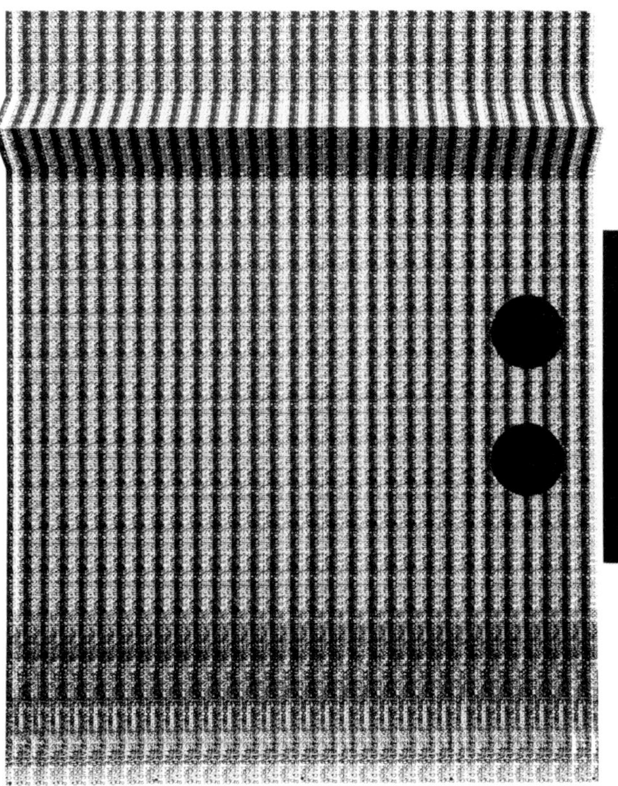

Y

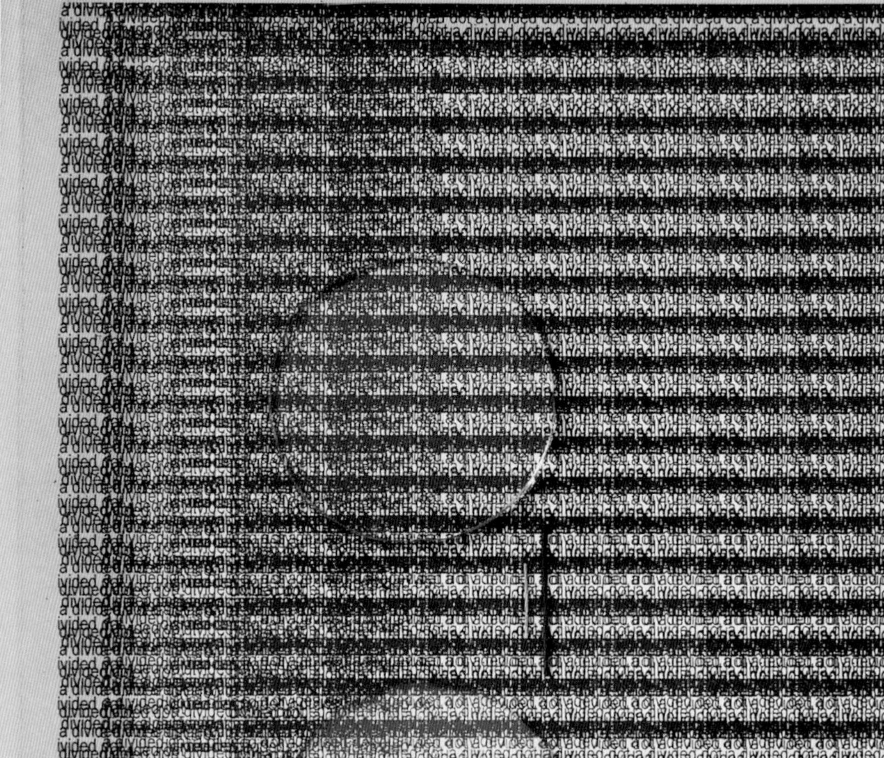

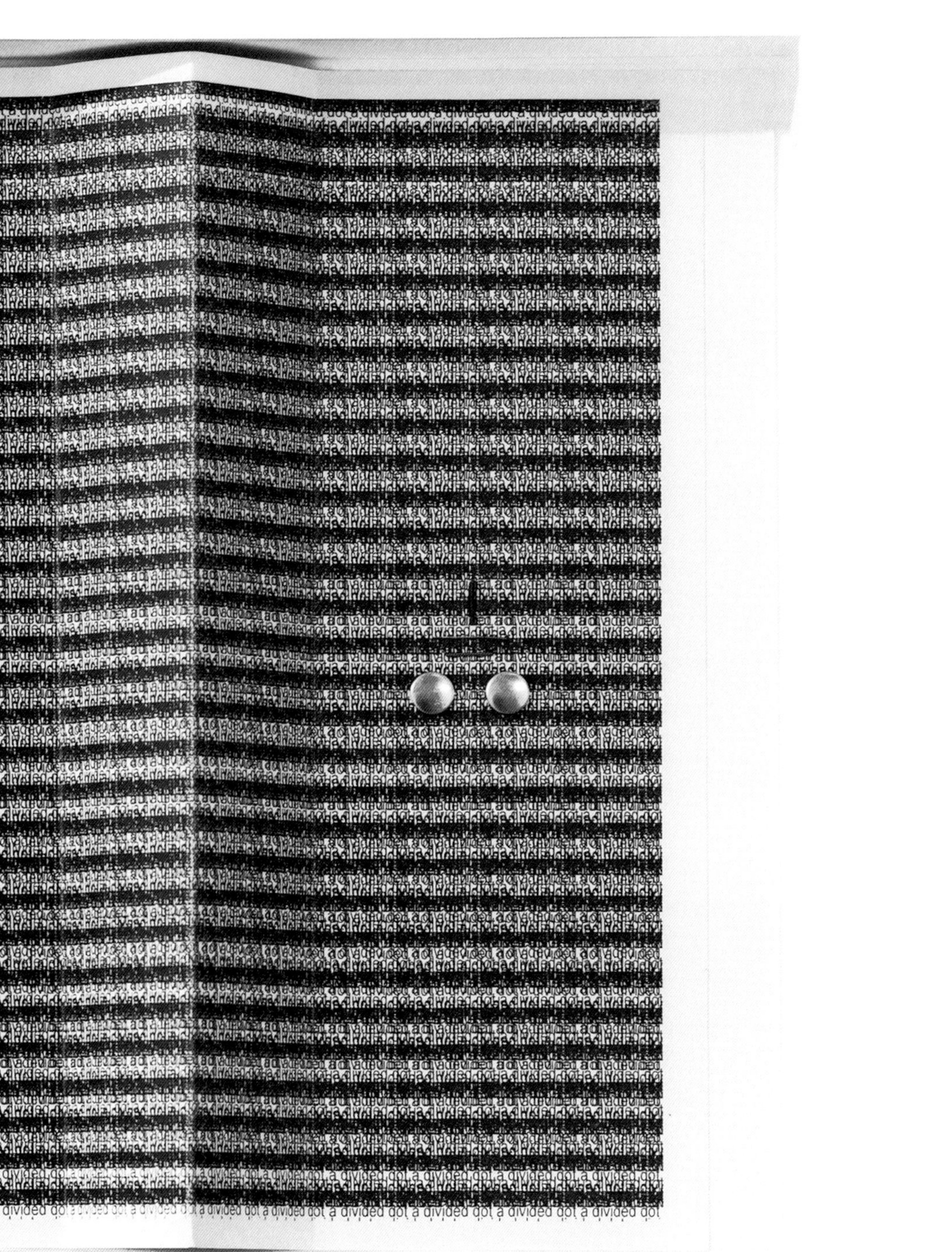

The Differential Mystery of Unprecedented Light
A Reading of Marlena Kudlicka's Works

Octavio Zaya

It is not very helpful, I believe, to place a contemporary work of art within a tradition of thought or a movement, or to try to find its most relevant influences, before explaining the work itself. Parallels in ideas or language with other artists or thinkers do not necessarily lead us to an understanding of the work. On several occasions, I have related an artist's series of works to the main subjects for which she might be known, and, in some instances, I may have compared them to other series of her works, but, in such cases, I have only managed, at best, to generate a confused understanding of the works at hand. I should say, however, that the task is not easy when we are approaching some artists who articulate their works through ideas, languages, multidisciplinary discourses, images, theories, abstractions, and variations that we cannot freeze into static symbols or any sort of standard reading. In the case of Marlena Kudlicka, the difficulties her works pose to the regular art viewer cause them to appear as seemingly hermetic images and languages that no art theories or schools of thought brought from outside her own body of work could help to open up.

Standards and errors are precisely the origins of the series of sculptures that Kudlicka has produced in Lima, Peru during her three months' residence there. She presents her works as if they were standard propositions - universally quantified claims - constructed from basic units analogous to the three sizes of units found in language and logic: those of words, sentences, arguments - these last (beliefs or judgments) being understood, in general, as the principal units of epistemology. But Kudlicka knows that linguistic, scientific, and philosophical understandings are not just a result of inductive associations from unadulterated perceptions. She knows that linguistic, scientific, and philosophical concepts are often significantly different from what we understand as common sense, and need to be formulated through difficult experimentation and theory formation, requiring new forms of thinking and mathematics and new regimes for experiment, checking, and proof. That is, this new thinking and new experimentation are strictly organized and controlled to minimize error.

This does not imply that we are dealing with a single theoretical perspective. As Steven Horst explains in relation to science, "Scientists use a number of distinct models: relativistic and quantum models, wave and particle models, evolutionary and molecular-genetic models. Like different types of maps, scientific models can be incommensurable with one another, have incompatible representational systems and background assumptions, and license contradictory predictions. This is one of the principal phenomena described as 'disunity of science.'"[1]

In the work I am most familiar with - particularly in the large-scale sculptures made of powder-coated steel and glass - Kudlicka is apparently complicating matters. According to the artist, the series ***f=different*** analyzes and verifies dependencies between the concept of "difference" and the notion of "standard," as well as the mutual relationship between them. "The title ***f=different*** refers to the transition through different states with incompleteness caused by error," the artist says: **f** is a durable unit, an axiom of uniformity in pattern and a constant function, while the **different** is a group of various elements of the same value, or an equivalence, which then tends to balance the invariability of the function **f.** According to the artist, the concept behind this proposition oscillates between contraries in modern endeavors such as Quality Control and Standard Verification.

In this set of sculptures, Kudlicka is reviewing the history of DIN A4 paper and how the idea of such a standard affected linguistic and behavioral mechanics. The ultimate interest of the artist is "What tolerance of precision is allowed to transform thought into a physical shape?" The question is already posed by the title of the work, which is of such a self-contained nature that it is hard to connect it with the subject of the work. But this difficulty is not primarily in following the argument, but rather in grasping the references of the language itself. Ultimately, Kudlicka uses mathematics, and science in general, as poetry rather than as an instrument of measure or to describe her subjects as physics sees them. She expands those units found in language and logic to include alternative models and "peripheral" processes, operating according to different, non-intentional, non-rational principles to produce other types of cognition and other types of composition. For "the standard" doesn't provide a reason to suppose that it supplies an adequate reading of the units of thought. For her, linguistics, science, and philosophy are modes of articulation to support speculative and poetic exercises in thinking through her ideas, in which errors are not simple characteristics of the object, but rather characteristics about its potential relation to the interests of the ideas: "Errors force us to go back to zero, to start over and try to reach this balance by either adding or subtracting elements."[2]

The reading of the work is, thus, as open as is the actual composition of the work - not so much because we could understand it as a concept-shape, but because its "tolerance for precision" creates a necessary gap between the work and what it represents, always implicating knowledge and always dogged by the history of the epistemological problems of language as representation. There is no centre or point to which to anchor the work, and yet there is a unity of the work within its own space; an optical and linguistic unity closed in itself and indifferent to its environment. In this, Kudlicka's work is not far from concrete poetry, from typographic representations, from some Constructivist architecture or even from some of the best works of her compatriot Katarzyna Kobro (1898–1951). In some cases, it uses points, letters, digits, and words, within interacting lines and volumes, to create what amounts to drawings in space. In other cases, it privileges some elements over others. But in all the cases, we could say that it arranges different forms of knowledge in its search for a potential, in its thinking through a form of thought.

But I am not just considering Kudlicka's form and structure as static entities. As the work becomes more concrete and synthetic, its internal unity, the spacing between elements, ceases to be an empty space (the empty space of transparent glass), and it does not rely on purely logical relations. We get to understand that those elements are used in many different ways, sometimes allowing more specific relations between the various elements of the work, as well as creating the possibility for internal reciprocity, recurrence, or circularity. Where we might expect the concrete form to be more closed, we find that its coalescence opens up the possibility of entering the work through its discontinuities. Even if Kudlicka suggests that the genesis of the work proceeds from the abstract to the concrete, from the idea (language or title) to the work, it should be noted that this process is not linear, and it is only possible through the discontinuous improvements (or errors) that make for the work being always changed or modified, although never in a continuous line.

From this account, some may infer that the "different" in the title of this series of works - a group of various elements of the same value, or an equivalence, which then tends to balance the invariability of the function **f** - may stand for the concept of difference as a foundational and constitutive principle. In other words, **f** would stand for the concept of traditional identity. And therefore, the understanding of identity would be that of the Differential ontology of Jacques Derrida and Gilles Deleuze. Through the history of thought, the essentialist tradition has located the identity of any given thing in some essential or self-contained properties (as in **f:** a durable unit, an axiom of uniform pattern, or a constant function). Differential ontology, however, understands the identity of any given thing as constituted on the basis of the ever-changing nexus of relations in which it is found, and, thus, identity is a secondary determination, while difference, or the constitutive relations that make up identities, is primary. Indeed, the relationship between the work and the concept of difference has already been recognized in another context.[3]

Whatever the readings and inferences elicited might be, Kudlicka's work does not follow a narrative or discursive thought. We can say the same about any poem: It is not a thought "as the explicit procedure of thought or as the thought that can be exposed only as thought,"[4] as in mathematics or philosophy. There is no clear link or singular deduction that traverses the work. The work "refers to [or is the result of] the transition through different states with incompleteness caused by error," as the artist says. Thus, Kudlicka's work is not a path but a threshold. This entrance into what Mallarmé called the mystery of unprecedented light[5] does not give away the key to understand it, and it does not help us to understand it, but it always compels us to think.

1 Steven Horst, *Cognitive Pluralism* (Cambridge, Massachusetts: MIT Press, 2016), p. 140.

2 Ruxanda Renita, "Interview with Marlena Kudlicka," http://artguideeast.com/right-news-feed/marlenakudlicka-artbaselmiami/, 2015 [Accessed 29 July 2016].

3 Somewhere in this book, Miguel von Hafe Pérez has pointed out that Kudlicka's work addresses the invisibility of women in the construction of the narratives of art history...

4 Alain Badiou, *Handbook of Inaesthetics,* trans. Alberto Toscano, ed. Werner Hamacher (Stanford: Stanford University Press, 2005), p. 19.

5 Stéphane Mallarmé, "Several Sonnets (I)/Plusieurs sonnets (I)," *Collected Poems,* trans. Henry Weinfield (Berkeley: University of California, 1994), p. 66.

Subtitle: Sculpture

Dorota Monkiewicz

Quality Control and Standard Verification is the title Marlena Kudlicka proposed for her exhibition at the Wrocław Contemporary Museum. Later, at my coercion, we agreed to add the subtitle "sculpture." Linguistic intuition tells us that this word, rooted in art history, resounds with more respect for artistic values than the prosaic and now-commonplace term "installation." Kudlicka's work, marked by a serious and investigative approach to art, seemed to require this (sub)titular framework for perceiving the exhibition.

In a technical sense, Marlena Kudlicka's pieces are installations, though they do not exist independently beyond the time frame of the exhibition. The various compositional elements, individually packaged, are stored in crates, which the artist herself designs with precision. The rebuilding of each work involves connecting and installing the various parts, which were tailor-made in the initial production stage. Assembling the works often does not even involve a screwdriver. The standing compositions are carefully balanced, which is why, for instance, the plate glass of the wheel in *unprotected 0 fig. 2* (2015) supports itself when placed alongside the metal construction.

In its strictest definition, a "sculpture" is a statue or a figure, a compact three-dimensional material form, subject to the force of gravity, which "stands" (it neither lies nor hangs), and above all, it maintains its balance. In the broadest sense, sculpture is "a work of art in a general sense," that can be transformed into a performance, installation, object, photograph, urbanistic project, or social action. Somewhere on this spectrum we find the art of the Polish Constructivist avant-garde - the spatial compositions of Katarzyna Kobro, and later, the early "interventions" of Edward Krasiński. They created "empty" sculptures, devoid of matter - vectors for navigating in space. In her private notes "*unprotected 0* series 2015 for abc Berlin," Marlena Kudlicka sketches a map of her intellectual and artistic inspirations, among which she names Wchutemas, Russian and Polish Constructivism, and Bauhaus. The formal attributes of works like *unprotected 0 fig. 2* (2015), or sculptural collages reveal evident links with the historical achievements of the avant-garde - the design of industrial objects (e.g. furniture) and functional print.

In Marlena Kudlicka's works in the *unprotected 0* series we also sense the atmosphere of the world of early modernity, from the 1920s and 30s. The technology used to produce her sculptures, created in a machine workshop and based on blueprints, hails from times when such repair workshops were an indispensable part of the industrial factories being built for the textile, machine, and heavy industries. These were the tools used by the artists of the first avant-garde. The ambitions of Bauhaus or Wchutemas, however, were to make individual prototypes that could go into mass production. According to the Modernist ideology, machine production meant depersonalized consistency and perfection.

Marlena Kudlicka has returned to the machine workshop with another intention. She adopts the avant-garde narrative, only to take it into a realm beyond the paradigm of anonymous and unified perfection. Her analytical reflection on the role of error in shaping a work of art is not far from Władysław Strzemiński's notion of the experimental nature of the artistic process. If unlike the Productivists, however, Strzemiński felt that the artistic process derived from the "emergence, the growth of the work," and not from reiterating the "structures of modernity," then to his mind this was in no way a conflicting process, in which could well appear an error or an unforeseen event that was accepted by the artist and incorporated into the work *a posteriori.*

The concept of error in Kudlicka's work is ambiguous and derives from the artist's hands-on approach to the sculptures in the workshop. This error can take the form of a simple oversight, or an unpredictable facet of the creative process, when she writes that, in general: "factors that affect the (physical and mental) shaping process include the observation of errors and their derivatives." Yet it can also concern another, more fundamental phenomenon. This is, on the one hand, a longing to achieve maximum precision, and on the other, the resistance of the material, the maximum limit of perfection in measurement and production tools. Between the nominal project parameters and physical enforcement parameters yawns a *terra incognita,* a crack in reality, a dimension that cannot be defined. This is a moment of pure potentiality, arising from the infinite capacity to divide a segment and the theoretical impossibility of dividing a point (the series entitled *a divided dot*) The artist's material sculptures are formed around this immaterial center, which can only be conceived through intellectual speculation. This grappling with the imperfection of a measurement created, for instance, [*unprotected 0* fig. 4]. This is an installation made of glass laboratory vials that went out of production owing to a slight imperfection in diameter. In order to remedy the lack of precision in these industrial products, Kudlicka prepared a separate, exclusive ring for each one, to hold them to the wall. Their precise and individual lathe production determines the sculptural aspect of this work.

The idea behind *unprotected 0* also draws from such a "crack in measurements," as the artist writes, that it is "a moment when one cannot yet surmise the future shape." "The title itself is, however, a sculpted text," she adds. Her work often leads us away from semantics and toward a graphic and spatial image of the text. A novelty in the *unprotected 0* series is the direct incorporation of the lines of a technical chart into the composition of the works. As Wikipedia asserts, "training is needed to be able to read and to understand technical drawings, but this is a language more precise and unequivocal than natural ones" (a quotation found in the artist's notebooks). This is not merely a question of precision, but also of the artist's mastering another means of communication, which has a practical significance as well, as she has to communicate with the contractor of the sculpture. Thus we return to the workshop, which the artist mythologizes as a place of mental and physical development of shapes. Marlena Kudlicka's Constructivist art operates in several intertextual fields: in language and its typographical image; in technical drawings and humanist speculation; in the engineering project; and in the intuitive correction of forms. This uncertainty in certainty, the identifying of the unknown in an objective and rational process, gives her work its utterly contemporary flavor.

The Measure of Decision

Miguel von Hafe Pérez

Whenever I happen to be in a city of any size, I marvel that riots do not break out every day: massacres, unspeakable carnage, a doomsday chaos. How can so many human beings coexist in a space so confined without destroying each other, without hating each other to death? As a matter of fact, they do hate each other, but they are not equal to their hatred. And it is this mediocrity, this impotence, that saves society, that assures its continuance, its stability. Occasionally some shock occurs by which our instincts profit; but afterward we go on looking each other in the face as if nothing had happened, cohabiting without too obviously tearing each other to shreds. Order is restored, a ferocious calm as dreadful, ultimately, as the frenzy that had interrupted it.

E. M. Cioran, *History and Utopia*

Imagine that we could quantify, with reasonable accuracy, the number of times that we're forced to take decisions, any decision, throughout a day. Imagine that this measurement could result in a graph on which we placed the decisions we've made on one side and our postponed decisions on the other. We can continue this speculative exercise, by thinking that it would be possible to go back and revisit the decisions that were frozen in a magma of non-events. Would our lives be any better? Would we be healthier and wiser, being able to decide from actual experience rather than from agonizing expectations? Or would we once again opt for the wrong decision? If we look at history, how often does this scenario seem to have been repeated?

Let's now think about the universe of creativity. A major part of the libertarian process of modernity seems to be precisely anchored in exploration of this magma of frozen decisions that when activated produce unexpected results. We merely need to consider one of the artistic expressions whose (de-)structuring is based precisely on this principle i.e. jazz. Improvisation - a vital concept in this musical genre - is the paradigmatic form of exploring (possibly) wrong decisions using a pattern that is (possibly) right.

It would be tedious to enumerate all the moments when the notion of failure was imposed as an ethical and aesthetic imperative in the creative positions of artistic movements and individual artists of the modern age. Nowadays, multiple artists are pursuing this topic more or less consistently, sometimes with a sense of naivety that borders on cynicism or, at worst, ignorance: how many hundreds of works of the type "diagonal structure resting on the corner" currently delight a market that is avidly seeking any rehash of arte povera, Minimalism, and the process art of the 1960s?

Marlena Kudlicka is fully aware of the risks she's running. Moving in a creative territory that revisits the Constructivist avant-gardes of the early twentieth century, the typographic renewal of this period, and the history of the invisibility of the female presence in the construction of the teleological and phallocentric narratives of yet unwritten art history, the artist is fully aware that the aesthetic opportunism of her specific condition (a woman, inscribed within the specificity of Polish art, currently reinventing itself, that has been systematically exploring the idea of error for a decade) can ruin everything. Making hers a particularly arduous path to cross.

In her projects we can foresee a systematic projection that fundamentally serves to contradict itself and to constantly mutate: somewhere between the composition and construction discussed by Moholy-Nagy, the artist is aware that the process of materialization of an idea is definitely transfigured when it comes into direct contact with a host of unforeseen events, surprises, deviations of protocol, that are inherent to work in the atelier - where many of the achievements are carried out by third parties - wherein the analogy between the atelier and a laboratory is perfectly understandable in this context.

The dynamics of the concrete relations between the works, as in the case of this proposal entitled *"unprotected 0"* is only experienced after it is placed in the space, in a determinant that precisely presupposes the importance of the in-between as a reference to an expanded view of sculpture: a space of perceptive and sensory crossing, a space of unstable balances, to the extent that they are always understood subjectively.

When the artist obliges herself to respect a conceptual systematization (she likes to call it protocols) she knows that she is more or less drastically reducing the number of decisions to be taken in the constructive and compositional process of her works. However, what seems to me more relevant here is the conceptual dimension that she brings to these projects. In fact, the presence of a script that the viewer can more or less explicitly access, instead of simplifying its hermeneutic accessibility, makes it even denser. It is therefore a strategy of concealment through explanation.

This oxymoron is rooted in that which makes this project as singular as it is surprising: the inability to create art on the basis of a fixed precept. In the fixed nature of the found form(s), the possibilities of materializing the negated concept are reiterated. Imagine how tragic it would be for the artist to find the right protocol: we might conservatively say that it would become an academicism of itself, or, in its most catastrophic form, a paralyzing failure.

When I stated that Marlena Kudlicka revisits certain aporias of the modern age, I wanted to reiterate this speculative dimension of a process that we know is reified as an open wound, which we continue to lick with meticulous diligence. But isn't this the most radical position that any artist clamors for? Over recent decades we have found ourselves in a state of unprecedented civilizational anxiety. From the digital hyper-transparency to the opacity of important social and political setbacks, we watch in disbelief as the processes of consolidation of the basic premises of an enlightened and universal modern age are undermined. Artists therefore have a greater responsibility in refocusing the processes of unparalleled conceptual speculation in the pragmatic issues of everyday life. Because from this figured void, the hope of a civilizational whole glows.

Cesare Pavese wrote an admirable note in his book *This Business of Living:* "There are people for whom politics is not a question of universality, but simply of self-defense." If we transfer this idea to the current state of art, one might state that Marlena Kudlicka is seeking universality (is there a more comprehensive and qualifying concept than the unfulfilled modernity?) in contrast to the legitimate defense of much of the art that is currently being produced? And thus is introduced one of the most controversial interpretations of her work. Yes, because she demands a protocol for understanding the possibility of political existence in her apparent dissociation from life as such. In other words, her outlook is political, because it isn't pamphleteering. That complexity acts as the synonym of the active resistance to the mediocrity and the prevalent commercialization of taste.

An Encounter with Marlena Kudlicka

Friedrich Meschede

Marlena Kudlicka seduces the viewer of her works in two different ways. First, by means of their titles, that is, by the linguistic metaphors, she seeks to explain the space-consuming works. At the same time, the installations naturally materialize a physical presence that pulls the viewer into the spell of the viewed.

The exhibition at the Żak | Branicka Gallery is entitled *the weight of 8.* If the number "eight" were also spelled out, the rhyme would immediately be visually enlightening. Yet, as a particularity of this spelling, one must actually say both "weight" and "eight" out loud in order to grasp the connection that doesn't persist in the rhyme scheme. The number "8" can be seen as a possible outline for the exhibition that consists of eight subunits, or, to express it literarily, it could be understood as eight chapters of a spatial dramaturgy that is only gradually made accessible. The layout of the invitation card even appears to be like the floor plan of a spatial disposition; letters of the alphabet are composed of lines, while black and different shades of gray give variety to the graphic appearance. These seek to visualize the as yet unseen installation as guidance for a testing ground of plastic events. The code to penetrate this order remains undeciphered, but it is possible to feel the interrelation between conceptualization and the physics of forms.

In any case, this concentration on the title reveals a crucial core in Marlena Kudlicka's work. She refers to concrete poetry, a generic term that can be ascribed to both literature and the fine arts and that, in turn, transforms the flowing transitions between the medium of language, its visualization using letters as a pictorial form, and sounds as concepts of rhythm into a complex system. The stiff guidelines of grammar turn into a new order through a playful disregard of grammatical regularity. The technique of collage used for concrete poetry consists of the combination of opposites and elements that would not initially be thought of as going together. The vocabulary of constructions creates the surprise.

At the time that this text was written, the exhibition did not yet exist. There was a sketch of the project from which it could be deduced that Marlena Kudlicka will arrange the gallery space by installing metal rods and plastic forms that appear like a drawing in space. The architecture of the space is simultaneously shell and point of reference.

Marlena Kudlicka proceeded in a similar fashion with her 2012 installation entitled *numbers minus letters* at the CGAC in Santiago de Compostela, or with the work *I lost a minute But gained a day*. Both titles are similar in that they present an absurd calculation. Letters cannot be subtracted from numbers and a lost minute is not equal to the entirety of a day. Nevertheless, these thought games stipulate various types of dimensions that suggest conceptual spaces; numbers allow for everything to be measured, and letters allow for everything to be depicted. But algorithms minus grammar send the viewer back to what he sees before him. In the case of Santiago de Compostela this consisted of forms and lines in space that were taken from the scale of the given architecture. Algorithms are a basic part of mathematics, which is itself, in the form of measurements and divisional proportions, an important aspect of architecture and its felt sense of space. The architect of the exhibition center in Spain is Álvaro Siza, who works in the international Modern tradition, in which abstraction is the inherent guideline. Marlena Kudlicka has implemented this into her three-part staging/production. An elongated rectangle that she placed in the center of the room by means of metal rods corresponds to a multi-piece wall installation whose parts look like typographic signs. The work on the floor depicts a measurement, while the work on the wall tells of signs. Common for both of them is a harmony in space that ascribes to each part its own existence. If there is a category of the Modern that distinguishes the perception of art in the twentieth century from that of earlier centuries, then it is the participation of the viewer, his taking part in the work, which is conceived as an opposite. This opposite, due to its overall structure, unleashes our motivity so that we move in the space, allowing us to deduce its meaning, and thus to conceive it.

In this tradition the works by Marlena Kudlicka function in a specific manner because her installations avoid a middle or center. From every position a different line of sight emerges, which, being of equal value with all of the other points of view, allows for a composition of all parts with each other.

Not dissimilar to this is the installation composed of three chapters: "I lost a minute," then "But," and lastly, "I gained a day." The proportional discrepancy between the period of time of a minute (as sacrifice) and that of a day (as gain) is expressed in the interplay between fragile, often linear signs and the capacity of the space in which the viewer moves. What sounds like a kind of linguistic distortion appears as a space-consuming formation in an exactly different way since the proportions are balanced and seek harmony and comparability of forms among themselves. The plastic intervention in the space remains stronger than the linguistic intonation of its description.

Marlena Kudlicka's work, with its non-objective abstraction, is situated in a long tradition of Constructivism that experienced a particular manifestation in Poland. Here, one should mention the work of the sculptor Katarzyna Kobro (1898-1951), who was the first to make the borders between sculpture and architecture fluid. Her constructions could be understood as both potential architecture and open spatial structures. Other works involve an instability that is also distinctive in Marlena Kudlicka's work. The tectonic aspect is questioned when it is understood as an expression of power. It is deployed as a balance between various forms that stop each other; the weight of one element affects the stability of the whole.

Herein lies a direct connection between the idea of a Constructivism today, as Marlena Kudlicka develops it, and the predecessors of this idea in Polish art history. Concrete poetry, collage, sculpture as interaction among lines, surfaces, and volumes are basic concepts of an abstraction that is still able to prompt fascination today because the promise of the avant-gardists of old have not been completely fulfilled. There still exists an open remainder of that abstraction that wants to be seen differently today and that must be seen in connection with the present. The fascination for measurements, proportions, surface, and line forms in interplay with one another proves, through the transformation of these concepts, that Marlena Kudlicka owns the artistic power to exploit the potential of Constructivism in a new way in order to enrich us with her abstraction.

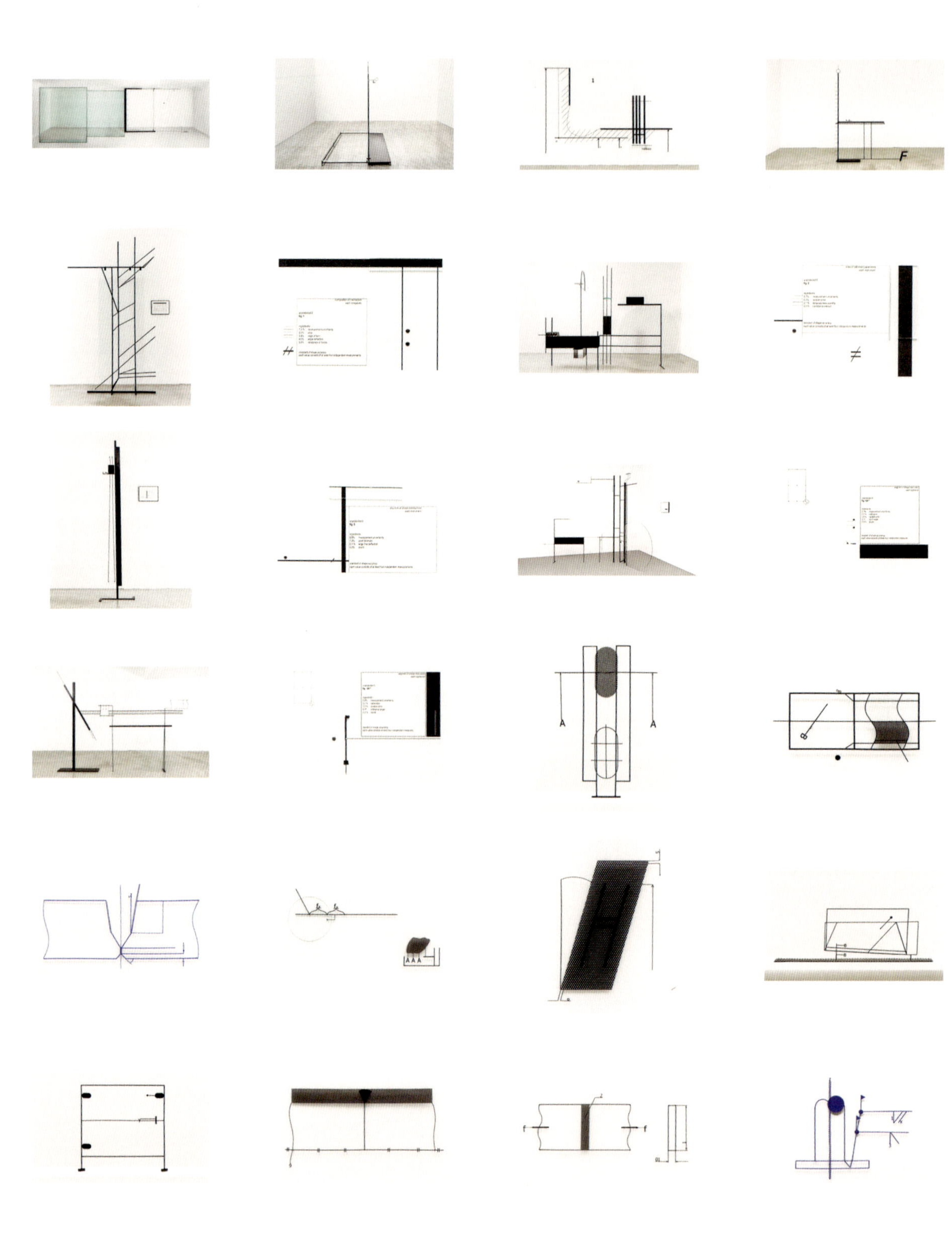

f=different version 8,5:A4
2016, sculpture
powdercoated steel
glass
730 x 235 x 163 cm
10 13 14 17 18

f=different f/To
2016, sculpture
powdercoated steel
glass
322 x 132 x 90 cm
20 22

f=different 9/9‘
2016, sculptural
composition on wall
powdercoated steel
glass
210 x 300 x 10 cm
24 27

f=different 3/1/1
2016, sculpture
powdercoated steel
glass
250 x 225 x 30 cm
28 31 32

unprotected 0 fig.1
2015, sculpture
powdercoated steel
glass
280 x 130 x 26 cm
39 45

unprotected 0 fig.1
2015, collage
print on paper, steel
glass
21 x 29,7 cm
39 41 45

unprotected 0 fig.2
2015, sculpture
powdercoated steel
glass
240 x 320 x 142 cm
42 44

unprotected 0 fig.2
2015, collage
print on paper
steel, glass
21 x 29,7 cm
44 47

unprotected 0 fig.3
2015, sculpture
powdercoated steel
glass
262 x 58 x 36 cm
49

unprotected 0 fig.3
2015, collage
print on paper
steel, glass
21 x 29,7 cm
49 51

unprotected 0 fig.120°
2015, sculpture
powdercoated steel
glass
240 x 177 x 137 cm
54

unprotected 0 fig.120°
2015, collage
print on paper, steel
21 x 29,7 cm
54 57

unprotected 0 fig.180°
2015, sculpture
powdercoated steel
glass
236 x 330 x 20 cm
58 61 62

unprotected 0 fig.180°
2015, collage
print on paper
steel
21 x 29,7 cm
62 65

shape hypothesis test A
2015, sculpture
powdercoated steel
54 x 36 x 2 cm
71

shape hypothesis test 0B
2015, sculptural collage
powdercoated steel
glass
25 x 57 x 4 cm
72

shape hypothesis test 5.1
2015, sculptural collage
powdercoated steel
75 x 41 x 4 cm
74

shape hypothesis test fx
2015, sculptural collage
powdercoated steel
glass
37 x 83 x 4 cm
76

shape hypothesis test H
2015, sculptural collage
powdercoated steel
45 x 62 x 5,5 cm
79

shape hypothesis test B
2015, sculpture
powdercoated steel
43 x 126 x 12 cm
80

shape hypothesis test Y
2015, sculpture
powdercoated steel
36 x 38,5 x 3 cm
82

shape hypothesis test 9
2016, sculptural collage
powdercoated steel
33,5 x 67,5 x 3 cm
84

shape hypothesis test f
2016, sculptural collage
powdercoated steel
28 x 63 x 3 cm
86

shape hypothesis test 1x
2016, sculptural collage
powdercoated steel
48 x 41 x 3 cm
88

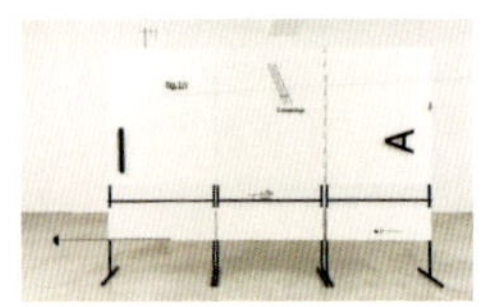

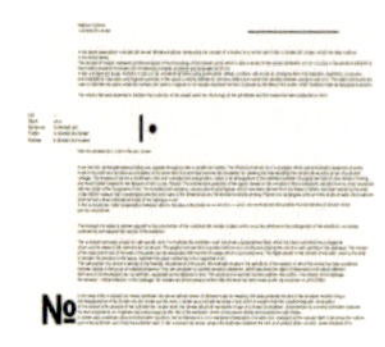

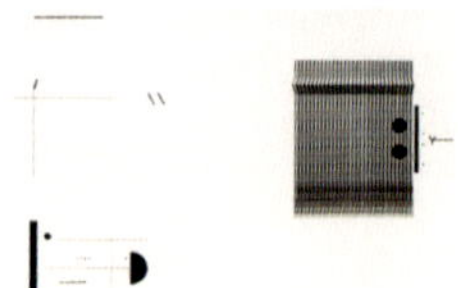

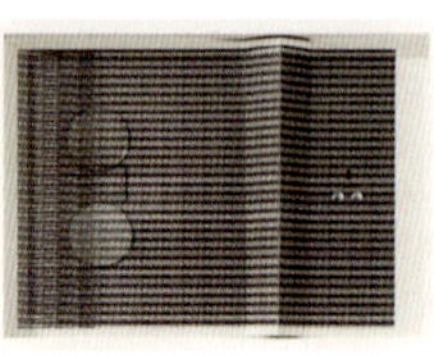

Lecture as a contour of A.
The beginning of shape
2015, sculpture
powdercoated steel
231 x 356 x 40 cm
94 96 98

a divided dot. review
2014, print
50 x 50 cm
104

a divided dot. folder
2014, sculptural
composition
powdercoated steel
print on paper
250 x 367 x 12 cm
106

a divided dot. N.01
2015, collage on paper
steel, glass, print
42 x 29,7 x 3 cm
108

Colophon

Concept

Marlena Kudlicka

Design

cmk.xyz

Authors

Friedrich Meschede
Dorota Monkiewicz
Miguel von Hafe Pérez
Octavio Zaya

Photo Credits

Marcus Schneider
Karina Ríos
Courtesy
The Artist
Revolver Galeria
ŻAK | BRANICKA

Image Processing

David Farfán

Proofreading

William Gilcher

Consultancy

Asia Żak Persons
Uta Grosenick

Edition

1500

ISBN 978-3-95476-172-2

Printed in Poland

Distribution

Gestalten, Berlin
www.gestalten.com
sales@gestalten.com

Translation:

Translator for Friedrich Meschede's text: Erika Pinner
Translator for Dorota Monkiewicz' text: Søren Gauger
Translator for Miguel von Hafe Pérez' text: Martin Dale

Copy Editing

Shao-Lan Hertel
Małgorzata Warmińska-Marczak
Octavio Zaya's text edited from the original English version by Amittai Aviram

Production Management

ŻAK | BRANICKA

Production

Zakład Poligraficzny
Moś i Łuczak
Poznań, Poland

Typeface

Akzidenz Grotesk

Paper

FocusArt Natural
135 g/m²

Published by

DISTANZ Verlag
www.distanz.de

Acknowledgments

Jacek Kowalski
Friedrich Meschede
Dorota Monkiewicz
Miguel von Hafe Pérez
Asia Żak Persons
Monika Branicka
Giancarlo Scaglia
Octavio Zaya

Supported by

ŻAK | BRANICKA
Revolver Galeria
MWW Wrocław
Contemporary Museum

Collections

Collection Castro Carregal, Spain, “shape hypothesis test B”, 2015, sculpture, 80
Jack Cohen Collection, Lima, “shape hypothesis test fx”, 2015, sculptural collage, 76
Collection Francisco Fino, Lisbon, “a divided dot. folder”, 2014, sculptural composition, 106
Galila’s Collection, Belgium, “a divided dot. N.01”, 2015, collage, 108
Sammlung Haus N, Kiel, “unprotected 0 fig.180°”, 2015, sculpture, collage, 58-65
Private Collection, Vienna, “shape hypothesis test A”, 2015, sculpture, 71
Giancarlo Scaglia Collection, Lima, “shape hypothesis test 0B”, 2015, sculptural collage, 72
Jacqueline Shor Collection, São Paulo, “shape hypothesis test 5.1”, 2015, sculptural collage, 74

ŻAK | BRANICKA

REVOLVER GALERIA

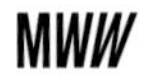

Wrocław
Contemporary Museum

numbers	minus	letters